D0095506

EVERYDAY LIFE
IN ANCIENT
EGYPT

BAKER COLLEGE OF
CLINTON TWP. LIBRARY

EVERYDAY LIFE IN ANCIENT EGYPT

JON MANCHIP WHITE

DRAWINGS BY HELEN NIXON FAIRFIELD

DOVER PUBLICATIONS, INC.
MINEOLA, NEW YORK

Copyright

Copyright © 1963, 1991 by Jon Manchip White
All rights reserved under Pan American and International Copyright
Conventions.

Bibliographical Note

This Dover edition, first published in 2002, is an unabridged republication of
the edition first published in 1963 by B. T. Batsford Ltd., London, and G. P.
Putnam's Sons, New York.

Library of Congress Cataloging-in-Publication Data

White, Jon Ewbank Manchip, 1924-
    Everyday life in ancient Egypt / Jon Manchip White ; drawings by Helen
Nixon Fairfield.
        p. cm.
    Originally published: London : Batsford ; New York : Putnam, 1963.
    Includes bibliographical references and index.
    ISBN 0-486-42510-X (pbk.)
    1. Egypt—Social life and customs—To 332 B.C. I. Title.
    DT61 .W48 2002
    932—dc21

                                                                2002031302

Manufactured in the United States of America
Dover Publications, Inc., 31 East 2nd Street, Mineola, N.Y. 11501

To the memory of
**THE LATE
S. R. K. GLANVILLE**
Herbert Thompson Professor of Egyptology
in the University of Cambridge

Friend and Teacher

CONTENTS

	Page
LIST OF ILLUSTRATIONS	9
ACKNOWLEDGMENT	13

I THE NILE VALLEY
The Character of the Valley	15
The Character of the People	17
The Sense of Continuity	20
The Earliest Settlers	25

II DWELLING PLACES
Towns and Cities	29
The Main Cities	32
Pyramids	39
A Visit to a Temple	49
Houses	64
Tombs	74

III THE HOME
Dress	87
Furniture	99
Food and Drink	103
Transport	108

IV PEOPLE AND PROFESSIONS
Pharaoh	113
Noblemen and Administrators	121
Priests	128
Soldiers	142
Scribes	151
Artists	152
Peasants	162

CONTENTS

V PRIVATE LIFE
   The Family   169
   Education   173
   Sports and Pastimes   181
CHRONOLOGICAL SUMMARY   190
BIBLIOGRAPHY   192
INDEX   193

THE ILLUSTRATIONS

The numerals in parentheses in the text refer to the
figure-numbers of the illustrations

Figure		*Page*
1	Map of Ancient Egypt	14
2	Egypt's great highway: the river Nile	16
3	The reluctant donkey: detail from a tomb-relief	19
4	The Narmer Palette	21
5	The central quarter of Tel el-Amarna	22
6	Huntsmen from the pre-dynastic period	25
7	Pre-dynastic objects	26
8	A pre-dynastic bead necklace	27
9	Earthenware pots and chest of the Fourth Millennium	27
10	A street scene in Tel el-Amarna	31
11	The god Ptah, patron of Memphis	33
12	The body of a rich man being brought to Abydos	35
13	Deir el-Bahri: the Temple of Queen Hatshepsut	36
14	Nubians bearing tribute	38
15	Group of *mastaba* tombs at Sakkara	40
16	Sectional view of the interior of a *mastaba*	40
17	The Step Pyramid, Sakkara	42
18	The Temple of Ramses II at Abu Simbel	43
19	The smaller temple at Abu Simbel	44
20	The Sphinx and the Pyramid of Chephren	44
21	The building of the Great Pyramid of Cheops	46
22	Obelisk at Karnak	48
23	A provincial nobleman inspects his cattle	50
24	A temple pylon	52
25	Map of the Thebes area	53
26	Girls carrying temple offerings	55
27	Temple of Amon-Ra at Karnak	57
28	Carpenters at work in the temple	59
29	Amon-Ra	63
30	Builders at work	65
31	A workman's house	67

32	The garden of a country villa	68
33	A villa	69
34	The central room of a villa	71
35	Alabaster lamp	72
36	A garden shrine	73
37	Anubis weighs the heart of a dead man	76
38	Detail from a Theban tomb painting	77
39	The chair of Tutankhamon	79
40	Mummy-case of a priestess	80
41	*Ushabti* of a woman holding a *Ba*-bird	80
42	*Ushabti* of Tutankhamon	80
43	A *ushabti* figurine	81
44	A room in a rock-cut tomb	83
45–6	Inlaid faience decorations	86
47	The White Crown of Upper Egypt	88
48	A razor	89
49	Men's and women's hairstyles	90
50	Full ceremonial dress	91
51	A princess's crown	92
52	Gold bangle, earrings and pendant	92
53	Part of a bead collar	93
54	Necklaces	93
55	Wooden toilet-case of Tutu	94
56	A nobleman	95
57	A bronze mirror	96
58	A perfume box	96
59	An elderly Nubian carrying an unguent vase	97
60	A maidservant	97
61	Bronze vessel	98
62	Wooden unguent spoon	98
63	Gold jug	98
64	Faience goblet	98
65	An ivory head-rest	100
66	Everyday furniture	101
67	Earthen pots and drinking vessels	103
68	Fig-picking	104
69	Forced feeding on a poultry farm	105
70	Grape-treading	106
71	A rich man and his wife at dinner	107
72	The nobleman Ti hunting hippopotami	109

73	A large boat under sail	110
74	Ramses II on his throne	114
75	Musicians and dancers: members of the royal *harîm*	116
76	Amenemhat III	119
77	The priest and royal scribe Hesira	120
78	The sage Imhotep, vizier of King Zoser	120
79	A vizier holding his *diwan*	124
80	A priest	128
81	Horus and his mother Isis	129
82	A priest and temple women in procession	132
83	Priests carrying a model of the sacred sun-boat	133
84	Isis, with her brother and husband Osiris	135
85	A granary	137
86	Ploughing	138
87	Milking	138
88	An offering to the dead	139
89	A priest completes the rite of mummification	141
90	Syrian captives	143
91	A two-horse chariot	147
92–3	Archers and spearmen on the march	148–9
94	A scribe	151
95	Sculptors	154
96	Wildfowling	157
97	Girl playing a harp	158
98	Female musician with a lute	158
99	A painter	161
100	A peasant hoeing	163
101	Harvest time: reaping and winnowing	165
102	A *shaduf*	166
103	Ladies in gala dress	170
104	A priest and his wife	171
105	Seated woman	172
106	Womanservant grinding corn	172
107	Mother and child	172
108	Writing equipment	174
109	Hieroglyphic alphabet and signs	177
110	Weighing gold	180

111	Boys wrestling	181
112	Hunting equipment	182
113	A hunting dog	183
114	A *mîw*	183
115	Girls at play	184
116	A game of draughts	185
117	An acrobat	185
118	Musicians at a banquet	186
119	Musical instruments	187
120	The blind harpist	189

ACKNOWLEDGMENT

The Author and Publishers wish to thank the following for permission to reproduce the illustrations appearing in this book:

Arts Council of Great Britain for figs 62–4 and 106

Ashmolean Museum, Oxford for figs 42 and 78

The Trustees of the British Museum for figs 40, 41, 61, 86, 97, 98, 104 and 105

Brooklyn Museum (Department of Ancient Art) for fig 107

Cairo Museum of Egyptian Art for figs 4, 39, 62–4, 76, 77, 87 and 106

Carlsberg Museum, Copenhagen for fig 85

Egypt Exploration Society and J. D. S. Pendlebury for fig 5 (from *The City of Akhenaton*, Vol. III)

Hachette, Arts du Monde, Paris for fig 96 (from *Les Chefs d'œuvre de la Peinture Egyptienne*)

Max Hirmer for fig 76

Lehnert and Landrock for figs 4, 39, 77 and 87

City of Liverpool Museums for fig 59

Metropolitan Museum of Art, New York for fig 60

Sidgwick & Jackson Ltd and Margaret Murray for fig 109 (based on plates XCVI and XCVII of *The Splendour that was Egypt*)

Roger Wood for figs 18–20

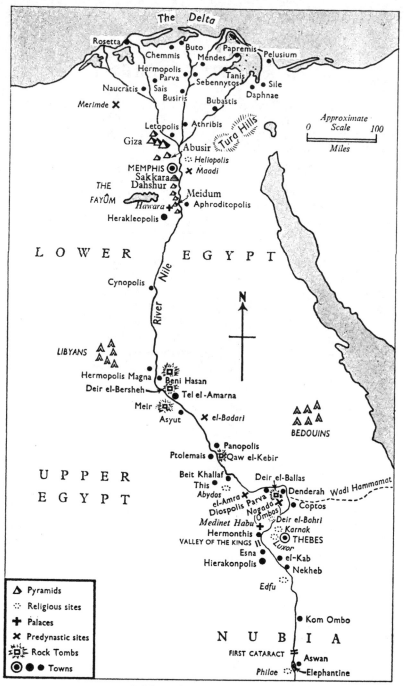

The Delta

Rosetta
Buto
Papremis Pelusium
Chemmis
Mendes
Hermopolis
Parva
Sebennytos
Tanis
Sile
Naucratis
Sais
Daphnae
Busiris
Bubastis
Merimde ✗
Letopolis
Athribis
Tura Hills
Giza ⟐
Abusir
∴ Heliopolis
MEMPHIS ◉
✗ Maadi
Sakkara
Dahshur △
THE
Meidum
FAYÛM
Hawara ✚
● Aphroditopolis
Herakleopolis ●

L O W E R   E G Y P T

River Nile

Cynopolis ●

N

Approximate Scale
0   100
Miles

LIBYANS

Hermopolis Magna ●
Beni Hasan
Deir el-Bersheh
Tel el-Amarna
Meir
Asyut
✗ el-Badari

BEDOUINS

Panopolis
Ptolemais ●
Qaw el-Kebir

U P P E R

E G Y P T

Beit Khallaf
This
Deir el-Ballas
Abydos ∴
el-Amra ✗
Denderah   Wadi Hammamat
Diospolis Parva
Nagada
(Ombos)
Coptos
Medinet Habu ✚
Deir el-Bahri
Hermonthis
Karnak
VALLEY OF THE KINGS
THEBES ◉
Luxor
Esna ●
el-Kab
Hierakonpolis ●
Nekheb

Edfu

△ Pyramids
∴ Religious sites
✚ Palaces
✗ Predynastic sites
⊡ Rock Tombs
◉ ● ● Towns

Kom Ombo ●

N U B I A

FIRST CATARACT
Aswan
Philae ∴
Elephantine

1 Map of Ancient Egypt

Chapter I

THE NILE VALLEY

THE CHARACTER OF THE VALLEY

THE ancient Egyptians were passionate gardeners and accomplished botanists; so it is fitting that the land in which they lived should have resembled the flower which they most loved to depict upon their monuments: the lotus.

If you look at the map of Egypt (opposite), you will see that it is like the spreading head of a flower set on a long thin stalk. The head is the fan-shaped Delta of the river Nile; the stalk is the swaying curve of the river as it unwinds its course from the First Cataract at Aswan to the distant Mediterranean. And the sap which gives life and vigour to the plant is the water of the Blue and White Niles, springing from their distant source in the heart of Africa, 4,000 miles from the sea.

With the exception of Chile, Egypt has the strangest contour of any country in the world. Most countries are round or square or elongated: but Egypt is a thread of wet green silk stretched loosely on an eternity of yellow desert.

The character and destiny of a country is controlled by its location, its conformation and its climate. Few countries have been so influenced by these factors as ancient Egypt. Egypt *was* the river Nile. It was a narrow carpet of soil enclosed within a rocky slot in the sands. The inhabitants of the valley huddled together on their magic carpet, which had been spread out for them by the benevolent gods at the beginning of the world; and they took good care not to stray from it. Who would be so stupid as to leave a happy valley, watched over by the gods, to wander among the demon-haunted wastes of Sinai or the Sahara?

Indeed, they had little cause to look beyond their own teeming strip of soil. If the mountains on each side of them were a barrier, they were also a protection. The land of Egypt was a blissful abode, 'a unique and enormous oasis, a garden in a

15

2   Egypt's great highway: the river Nile

wilderness'. The sun shone down with a soft warmth and steady radiance. The mighty river spilled its waters over the fields and plantations for over 100 days in every year, laving the earth with a nourishing tilth from the uplands of Abyssinia. The soil of Egypt was so fertile in texture and so dark in colour that the ancient Egyptians called their country *Kemet*, the *Black Land*, to distinguish it from the *Red Land*, the arid desert in which it was situated.

No wonder that they praised their river, worshipped it, sang to it such sweet hymns as *The Adoration of the Nile*. 'Praise to thee, O Nile, that issueth from the earth, and cometh to nourish Egypt. Thou art verdant, O Nile, thou art verdant. He that maketh man to live on his cattle, and his cattle on the meadow! Thou art verdant, thou art verdant; O Nile, thou art verdant.'

The ancient Egyptians were river-dwellers. They were born, lived and died on the banks of the maternal expanse of water which filled any traveller who came to gaze upon it with feelings of awe and wonder(2). Nor did it merely provide them with their daily sustenance: it yoked them together into a single powerful nation. It was the highway which united the stony uplands at the southern end of the lotus with the lush lands of the Delta, where the river suddenly braked and broke into a thousand filaments before it oozed its way through the marshlands to the sea. The uplands (at the lower end of the map) were originally known as the kingdom of Upper Egypt; while the Delta, whose boundary

16

began ten miles upstream of ancient Memphis, was called the kingdom of Lower Egypt. The two kingdoms originally existed as two loose but distinct confederations of tribes for more than a thousand years; but it was inevitable that with the steady growth of population they should sooner or later coalesce, an event that occurred a little later than 3000 B.C., shortly before the beginning of the First Dynasty. Yet each kingdom still retained its own individuality. The men of Upper Egypt, where the terrain was rugged and severe, tended to be fierce and somewhat puritanical. The men of Lower Egypt, on the other hand, were mild and easy-going; they dwelt in rich and placid surroundings, within reach of the cultured lands of the East Mediterranean.

THE CHARACTER OF THE PEOPLE

Until a late stage in Egyptian history, even the lowlanders of the Delta had only limited contact with the outside world. True, there had always been an import trade in oil, wood and jewellery from such civilised countries as Syria, Crete and Phoenicia; but the trade with the savage lands of Nubia and the Sudan was equally extensive. In any case, trade with foreign countries was almost entirely a royal prerogative, and thus limited in its cultural impact.

From the beginning of their history, the people of Egypt were notorious stay-at-homes. They were markedly less curious about their neighbours than their neighbours were about them. Thus, different as the folk of Upper Egypt might be from the folk of Lower Egypt, to the eye of the foreign visitor they were almost indistinguishable from each other, and were certainly quite unlike the citizens of any other land. From their earliest formative years the Egyptians had been shut away from the rest of the world. They had worked out their own way of life for themselves without much regard for other societies. They had grown up in isolation.

It is this shut-in, almost claustrophobic atmosphere which, although one must not exaggerate it too much, lends ancient Egypt its unique character. The Egyptians were not men like other men—eager to welcome new ideas from abroad. (It is curious, for example, that although it is generally assumed that the horse was not introduced into Egypt until the Eighteenth

Dynasty (c. 1700 B.C.), a horse's skeleton was found by Professor Emery in 1959 at the Egyptian fortress of Buhen in Nubia, buried in a rampart of Middle Kingdom date. Thus the Egyptians knew about the horse—perhaps used by their nomadic enemies—at least 200 years before they decided to adopt it for riding. Why did they choose to ignore it? In the absence of further evidence it would be foolish to speculate too intensively. But might not their temperamental conservatism have played some part in it? They possessed their own strange and stubborn notions of how life should be conducted. As we have said, they were 'oasis dwellers', denizens of a hidden cleft in the gritty wastes of the North African plain. Except for a period rather late in their history, when they ventured out of the valley to lord it over a large swathe of the Near East, the great world more or less passed them by. And even this belated experiment in imperialism seems to have been prompted more in order to establish forward defence-lines rather than to found an empire. If the world passed them by, they were perfectly content that it should do so.

Not that they were in any sense backward or undeveloped: they were merely set apart. Indeed, in many respects their way of life was held by their neighbours to be superior to every other in the ancient world. They were envied for their serenity, their industry, their discipline. They can claim to have been one of the least neurotic civilisations that the world has seen. Their geographical isolation was so extreme that until a late stage in their history they were spared the ordeal of constant foreign invasion; and coupled with the absence of anxiety that goes with freedom from being conquered, they lacked the miserable sense of guilt that blights the spirit of the conqueror.

They were not aggressive; they were content to enjoy the peaceful seclusion of their sun-saturated valley. Feeling secure, they were able to evince a stable and sensible attitude towards the vicissitudes of life. Calmness and wisdom are the fruits of undisturbed meditation, and the ancient Egyptians were certainly calm and wise to an exceptional degree. The Egyptologist, J. A. Wilson, refers to the 'sense of confidence, assurance and special election' in the life of the ancient Egyptians, and speaks of the 'characteristic cheerful urbanity' of their mode of existence (*The Burden of Egypt*, p. 143). Another scholar, Sabatino Moscati,

18

3 The reluctant donkey: detail from a tomb-relief

contrasts the Egyptian temperament, which was so frank and so open, with the chronic state of mental dread in which the Mesopotamians spent their days. He speaks of the Egyptians' 'gaiety and prosperity', of their 'smiling outlook on life, their taste for laughter and jest which were unknown to the other peoples of the ancient Orient' (*The Face of the Ancient Orient*, pp. 99 and 148).

The old notion that the Egyptians were a prim, solemn and joyless set of people, frozen like the figures on their monuments into cramped attitudes, is quite false and unjustified. It is only on a superficial plane that the frescoes and reliefs of ancient Egypt seem so frigid and formal. A closer look at them will reveal that they almost always possess a host of sly details betraying an irresistible sense of fun(*3*). As Pierre Montet, one of the most celebrated of modern Egyptologists has put it, 'We can no longer accept the picture of the Egyptians as a horde of slaves impotent before the whims of a merciless Pharaoh and a bigoted and rapacious priesthood. For the ordinary Egyptian, the good moments of life outnumbered the bad.' (*Everyday Life in Egypt in the Days of Rameses the Great*, p. 330.)

This book will serve a useful purpose if it helps to dispel any impression of prevailing gloom that readers may have been previously tempted to form with regard to the ancient Egyptians. They were relaxed, tolerant, and filled with an appetite for

19

life; and they can boast that their history is utterly free from the barbarous blemishes that disfigure the reputations of many other otherwise intelligent and commanding peoples. (Read, for example, the section entitled 'Shows and Spectacles' in F. R. Cowell's *Everyday Life in Ancient Rome*, pp. 169–79, in this series.)

<h2 style="text-align:center">THE SENSE OF CONTINUITY</h2>

We are going to examine, in the pages that follow, the various aspects of everyday life in ancient Egypt. But to what extent, you may object, can one legitimately refer to 'everyday life' in a civilisation which lasted for tens of hundreds of years? Surely the 'everyday life' of the New Kingdom must have differed at almost every point from the 'everyday life' of the Middle Kingdom, just as that of the Middle Kingdom must have differed from that of the Old Kingdom?

Most of the other books in this series deal with a restricted span of time: a few centuries, perhaps a millennium. In the case of ancient Egypt, we must consider a vast stretch of social history, extending for more than 3,000 years. At least 30 centuries separate King Menes, the founder of the First Dynasty, from Nectanebo II, the last of the native Pharaohs. And from the close of the reign of Nectanebo II, at the end of the Thirtieth Dynasty, there were still three centuries to run before the birth of Christ.

Thirty dynasties. When King Nectanebo cast his mind back to his predecessor, King Menes, it was as though we, in our own lifetime, were to cast our minds back to the time when northern Europe had barely reached the mid-point of the Bronze Age. Between then and now Britain has been ruled by the Celts, the Romans, the Saxons, the Normans, and the dynasties that followed them. How then could we possibly undertake, in the space of a single book, to cover the subject of 'everyday life' in Britain? Equally, how can we hope to do so in the case of ancient Egypt?

Of course, the history of Egypt, even if it was more tranquil than that of Babylonia or Assyria, naturally underwent its ups and downs. Not even the most peace-loving civilisation can expect to dream through 3,000 years in complete and unalloyed passivity. We know that the calm of Egypt was violently disturbed

4 The victorious king Narmer raising his mace against a prisoner
Reverse of a slate palette from Hierakonpolis, First Dynasty

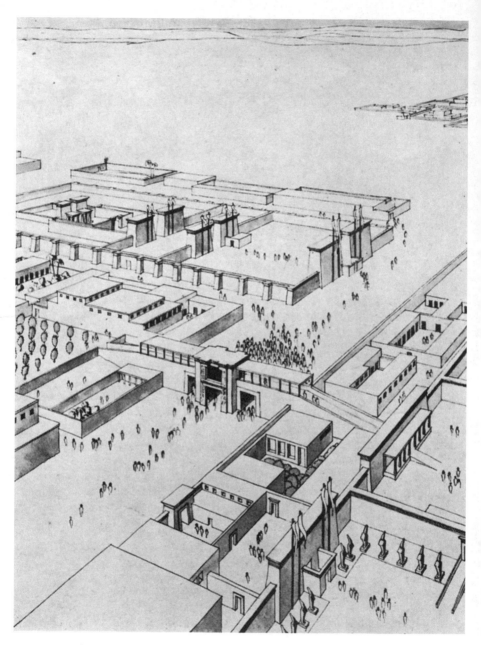

5 Reconstruction of the central quarter of Tel el-Amarna

by at least two great epochs of breakdown and strife: the First Intermediate Period, which divided the Old from the Middle Kingdom, and the Second Intermediate Period, which divided the Middle Kingdom from the New. 'Changes take place', complained the scribe Khekheppera of a period of upheaval:

> It is not like last year, and one year is more burdensome than another. The plans of the gods are destroyed and their ordinances transgressed. The land is in misery, mourning is in every place, towns and villages lament. All people are transgressors. The back is turned upon respect.

During such troubled epochs the citizens of Egypt tasted the bitter cup of exhaustion and civil war. Their secluded valley could shelter them from some of the ills that afflicted more exposed societies: but it could not shelter them from them all.

It is very remarkable, nevertheless, that the disasters of the Intermediate Periods affected the essential basis of Egyptian life only in a rather limited way. These periods did not wrench apart the entire framework of society; they did not disrupt the basic pattern. The Egyptians were deeply attached to their native traditions; and when an era of discord was over they rapidly returned to their former, friendly mode of life. We have mentioned the factors that gave to the Egyptians their sense of stability and optimism. It was this sense that helped them to set the ship of state back on an even keel when the hurricane had blown itself out.

They were also buoyed up by their profound and genuine admiration for their own past. They were more fanatical ancestor worshippers than the Shintoists of classical Japan. The Egyptians of the New Kingdom were as deeply stirred as any modern traveller by the sight of the pyramids of Giza, built when their world was young(20). They gloried in the achievements of their far-distant past. It is one of the curiosities of history that at the close of the dynastic epoch the Pharaohs of the Saite dynasty set themselves to copy the art and architecture of the mighty race of pyramid builders which had flourished 2,000 years before. It is as though the British desired to hark back to the style not of their Victorian or even Elizabethan forbears, but to the togas and sandals of the days when Britain was a Roman colony. Yet the proposal of the Saite kings was less bizarre than it may appear. The mode of life of Saite Egypt had not changed in any unrecognisable way from the mode of life of 2,000 years earlier. There was an irrefutable continuity. There had been certain interior shifts and adjustments; but the exterior surface was much the same. In this sense, therefore, we can speak quite truthfully of the 'everyday life' of ancient Egypt: an amiable, largely unexciting existence that endured more or less unchanged for an unbelievably protracted stretch of time.

The ancestor worship of the ancient Egyptians was closely bound up with their conception of the Golden Age. To most of the advanced nations of the world today the Golden Age lies in the future. The life of the present day is held to be simply a preparation for the happier and more glorious life which our children's children will live in a world free from want and war. This notion of a better life—which often degenerates into the facile notion of life as a kind of holiday from life—is, of course, closely bound up with the Christian notion of paradise. In turn, the Christian notion springs from the tenets of Hebrew philosophy, which have permeated Western thinking through the powerful influence of the Bible. Today even our conservatives profess to believe in, or at least pay lip-service to, the common aspiration for 'jam tomorrow'. The ancient Egyptians, on the other hand, did not torment themselves by comparing their present lot with the rosy paradise which they might enjoy if only they introduced pensions and welfare services and abolished the armed forces. Their Golden Age lay not in some hypothetical future, but was anchored in their past, when the gods themselves had reigned upon earth. Their beautifully balanced social system had been a precious gift from on high, and all that men were required to do was to try to hold the balance with steady grasp. Their object was not, as ours so often is, to transform their social system: they wanted to tamper with it as little as possible. They considered that all change was perilous, as it took society further away from the times when the good gods, after a long hard struggle with their enemies, had ruled so wisely over the valley. It is not surprising, therefore, that 'no people has ever shown a greater reverence for what was termed by them "the time of the ancestors" or "the time of the gods"' (Sir Alan Gardiner, *Egypt of the Pharaohs*, p. 56). The Egyptians held that

24

what a man ought to do was not to nurture 'progressive' ideals, but to put himself in tune with the rhythm of the universe as it had been established by the gods 'on the first occasion'. As Henri Frankfort puts it, 'The life of man, as an individual and even more as a member of society, was integrated with the life of nature, and the experience of that harmony was thought to be the greatest good to which man can aspire' (*Ancient Egyptian Religion*, p. 29).

Life for the Egyptians was here and now. According to King Pittakos of Mytilene, the secret of happiness lies in 'doing the present thing well'. The Egyptians observed this precept, and they were happy. The patient, craftsmanlike quality of everything they made—from first to last—is a testimony to it.

THE EARLIEST SETTLERS

The 'everyday life' with which we shall be dealing is that of dynastic Egypt between 3200 and 341 B.C. But dynastic Egypt did not spring into existence fully formed. It was preceded by a long pre-dynastic epoch which occupied at least 2,000 years before the first recorded Pharaoh appeared on the scene.

These pre-dynastic villagers, who had settlement sites in both Upper and Lower Egypt, gradually achieved a very high degree of civilisation. They were clever and sophisticated folk who laid the foundations of the flourishing Egyptian state that was to come. Their mode of life was sufficiently comfortable for the later Egyptians to be able to picture their blissful Golden Age as falling within this obscure epoch. Already, 2,000 years before

6 Huntsmen from the pre-dynastic period

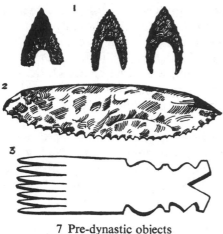

7 Pre-dynastic objects
1 Arrowheads   2 Serrated knife-blade
3 Comb of bone

the onset of the First Dynasty, the inhabitants of the Nile Valley had begun to evince those settled and leisurely characteristics which their descendants esteemed so highly. In the Fayûm and at Deir Tasa in Lower Egypt, and at such sites as el-Badari, el-Amra and Nagada in Upper Egypt, these nomads and pastoralists slowly absorbed the arts of agriculture. They grew barley and stored it in silos in the ground neatly lined with matting; they could sew and weave; they were expert boatmen; they could cook and bake; they manufactured a wide range of attractive combs, beads and bracelets; they used oils and unguents and painted their eyes with a cosmetic made from green malachite. Besides hunting with spears and arrows, which they tipped with skilfully shaped barbs of bone and flint, they kept cattle and goats, sheep and pigs, and had domesticated the cat and the wild dog.

By 4000 B.C. these talented villagers had already made many notable cultural advances. In particular, they had learned the secret of working copper. From about this date onwards the movement towards a closely-knit system of government, embracing both Upper and Lower Egypt, gathered irresistible momentum. The tribes, in their loose confederations, had reached the point where they were ready to coalesce. The prime impulse towards unification seems to have come from the African rather than the Mediterranean element in the population, from Upper rather than Lower Egypt. We have already noted that the men of the African highlands tended to be more bellicose than the folk of the Delta. The Upper Egyptians also controlled the head-waters of the river, and hence the water supply. They could therefore make the Delta-dwellers dance to their tune. All through Egyptian history it was the Upper

8 A pre-dynastic bead necklace

Egyptians who set the pace, and who showed themselves ready to rescue the country whenever it was pitched into one of its troughs. They were sticklers for ancient tradition, the watch-dogs of the Egyptian conscience. On the other hand, the men of the Delta were more inventive and adaptable, being open, as we have seen, to the bustling world of the Mediterranean. It was through the Delta that the skills of Hither Asia—for example, pictographic writing, ship-building and metallurgy—spread among the communities that bordered the Nile.

Figures 7–9 show a selection of the objects which these earliest Egyptians of the prehistoric or pre-dynastic period were accustomed to handle during the course of their everyday life. In particular there are examples of the superb flint knives which they chipped for ceremonial purposes; of the gaily decorated earthenware which they made in a wide repertoire of styles; of the exquisite jars and vases which they carved in an immense variety of different rocks and stones; of their personal orna-ments; and of their weapons.

9 Earthenware pots and chest of the Fourth Millennium B.C.

27

Chapter II

DWELLING PLACES

TOWNS AND CITIES

TIME, which has dealt gently with so many relics of ancient Egypt, has nevertheless behaved harshly towards her towns and cities. The statues, personal possessions and mummified remains of her rulers and citizens have been lapped in the warm sand for later generations to unearth. Not so the walls and towers of the teeming cities in which many of them passed their lives.

In the waterlogged terrain of the Delta the erosion of most of the old architecture was only to be expected. Lower Egypt also suffered from the disastrous activities of those human termites known as the *sebakheen*. The *sebakheen*, active during recent centuries, are the peasants who hunt for *sebakh*, the name that they give to the decomposed mud brick of ancient buildings which they dig up and use as fertiliser for their fields. In the drier domains of Middle and Upper Egypt, on the other hand, the principal destruction has been brought about simply by the casual dismantling of the early townships in order to erect later buildings—just as in England one sees blocks from ancient abbeys incorporated in the fabric of the neighbouring barns and farm-houses. One should also mention the ferocious, fanatical havoc wrought by the Coptic monks of the early Christian era. With chisel and sledge-hammer, these simple and misguided souls wandered the length of the land, hacking the heads and limbs off the statues and defacing the inscriptions of the 'pagan' pharaohs. They devoted years of their lives to this appalling task, and did their job only too thoroughly.

The surviving monuments of ancient Egypt, numerous as they appear to the modern traveller, represent an insignificant part of what originally occupied the ground. Of the once-proud cities of the pharaohs almost nothing is left. The temples, tombs, pyramids and colossi that still loom above the landscape are no more than the broken ribs of a long-dead giant. There is an air of gaunt isolation about these remains that has helped to nurture the legend that the men who built them must have been a race of humourless geometricians. This is far from being the case. These abandoned buildings were once embedded in a mass of dwellings of all sizes and descriptions. The towns and cities of ancient Egypt evidently possessed a great deal of the noise, smell, colour and general liveliness of the oriental bazaar, and the men who inhabited them were an active and exuberant breed.

Had you visited Thebes, Memphis or Tel el-Amarna, you would have found yourself plunged into a cheerful, sprawling, busy world(*10*). The obelisks and pinnacles were there, of course —not chipped and battered as they are today, but sleek and smooth and gleaming. And in those days they could only be sighted by peering over high encircling ramparts or through a living, leafy screen of palms and acacias.

The towering main buildings were like dignified islands standing up in the middle of a bustling ocean of less pretentious structures. True, the more prosperous members of the community usually lived in spaciously laid-out suburbs, as they do in modern cities; but the irrepressible flood of common humanity tended to seep and spread itself in its usual cheerful way into every available nook and cranny. Thus the imposing walls of some royal mortuary would be disfigured by an untidy collection of shacks and lean-tos, clinging to them like barnacles to the sheer sides of a stately liner. Occasionally a pharaoh or high priest would embark on a campaign to clean up the sacred precincts, and the interlopers would be summarily ejected. But the improvement tended to be temporary. As soon as the country entered its next period of anarchy or lazy government, the humble folk came inching back again to raise their huts hard up against the city's central buildings. Their instinct was sound. In normal circumstances the gates of the city were never shut either by day or night; but in times of emergency it was comforting to know that the protecting walls were close at hand. Also the palace or temple was the hub around which the commercial life of the town revolved, and it was common sense to edge as close as one could to the main source of wealth and patronage.

10 A street scene in Tel el-Amarna

THE MAIN CITIES

Let us imagine that we are Greek explorers who are visiting Egypt in its late and prosperous days. What cities would we have seen during our voyage from the Mediterranean seaboard to the Abyssinian highlands?

Entering the Delta through one of its many mouths, we would find that most of the larger townships there were mainly religious in character. In the middle of the marshes, bathed in a mysterious and wavering green light, our boat would float past majestic shrines dedicated to the principal Egyptian gods. Chief among them were the gods and goddesses who figured in the theological doctrines of the powerful priests of Memphis, or the dynasts who had made that mighty city their capital. At Buto and Sais were worshipped the cobra-goddess Edjo and the hunting-goddess Neith (the Egyptian Diana). Both these ladies had been venerated as long ago as the pre-dynastic epoch which was described at the end of the last chapter. Also in the Western Delta we would visit the town of Naucratis, which in later times became a flourishing port, forerunner of the great Greek city of Alexandria, afterwards the second city of the Roman empire.

Among the towns of the central Delta that we would probably choose to visit, if we had enough time, would be Busiris, the home of Osiris, most potent of all the gods; Athribis, Leto-polis; and Sebennytos; and, further to the east, Bubastis, sacred to the cat-goddess Bast; Mendes, devoted to the cult of the ram-headed god Khnum; and the important port of Tanis, which on several occasions had been fated to play a guiding part in pharaonic affairs. We would notice that the eastern and western rims of the Delta, which were naturally sensitive to incursion by outsiders, were systematically guarded. Here well-equipped battalions of troops were permanently stationed in large numbers and at permanent readiness.

The western frontier of the Delta was not threatened as seriously as its eastern counterpart. The potential invaders from the west merely consisted of marauding bands of Libyans and other tribesmen; but the eastern marches sat astride the high-road that led to the highly-organised kingdoms of the Hittites, the Syrians, the Mittannians, the Assyrians, and all the other peoples of the Near East who at one time or another cast covetous eyes at the land of Egypt. If we ventured beyond Tanis, into the heavily guarded military zone, we would discover that the most formidable of the chain of fortresses which covered this vulnerable sector of Egypt's boundaries was situated at Tjel or Sile (modern el-Qantarah). Here every traveller who entered or left Egypt was stopped for questioning by frontier guards, and his passport and credentials thoroughly checked.

Moving on upstream, near the point where the Nile divided into the two principal streams that flow through the Delta to the sea, we would soon sight the ancient and celebrated town of Heliopolis, now buried beneath the northern suburbs of Cairo. During the course of the Old Kingdom the priests of Heliopolis exercised a unique authority over the kings of Egypt. They elevated to supreme heights the cult of the sun god Ra and his gentle and much-beloved wife, the Cow-goddess Hathor, Lady of Heaven, Earth and the Underworld. The cult of Ra, in his twin guises of the wise old man Ra-Atum and the vigorous young falcon-god Ra-Harakhte, gave rise to the so-called Doctrine of Heliopolis. In consequence, it was inevitable that

the Doctrine should establish itself at the royal city of Memphis, situated no more than 26 miles to the south on the other bank of the river.

One of the Egyptian names for Memphis was *Hikuptah*, 'Mansion of the Soul of the God Ptah', a local god of great antiquity whose devotees thought that he had created even the sun-god himself. It may have been the word *Hikuptah*, later transformed into its rough Greek equivalent of *Aigyptos*, that was responsible for giving us the modern name of *Egypt*. As early as the beginning of the First Dynasty, about 3100 B.C., Memphis was already a centre of civilisation. There the conquerors from Upper Egypt had established an important palace, girt with the famous 'White Wall'. And 400 years later the great King Zoser of the Third Dynasty made it the official capital of the kings of Egypt.

11 The god Ptah, patron of Memphis

BAKER COLLEGE OF CLINTON TWP. LIBRARY

For the next five centuries, while Greece was still a wilderness, Memphis was the home of the mighty pharaohs of the Old Kingdom who, in the opinion of many scholars, brought the realm of Egypt to the unsurpassed peak of its power and prestige. It was a token of the greatness of Memphis that these early pharaohs built their pyramids on the high ground immediately to the west of it. The remains of no less than 19 of them can be traced, including the awesome group at Giza and the Step Pyramid of King Zoser himself(*17*). Five miles west of Memphis, we foreign visitors would be able to gaze at the fantastic Serapeum, an enormous underground tomb devoted to the ceremonial interment of sacred bulls. The mummified remains of 64 of these so-called Apis bulls, embodying the virtues of the gods of Memphis and Heliopolis, were solemnly buried there during a span of more than 1,000 years.

But now we must embark on a long, slow, leisurely row upstream against the pulse of the river.

We make a detour to pass a day at the old and influential provincial city of Herakleopolis, which for two brief spells was the leading city in Egypt without ever managing to establish itself as the actual capital. Then we are off again for a brief stop at This, the cradle of the dynasts who yoked together the prehistoric Egyptians into the Two Kingdoms. And finally we reach our principal objective, 250 miles upstream from Memphis: the much-venerated city of Abydos.

Here we have come to witness the most impressive of all Egyptian religious ceremonies, the annual performance of the mysteries of Osiris, which we shall be describing in a later chapter. Originally Abydos ranked after Busiris in the Delta as Osiris' second city, then gradually came to the forefront as the chief of Egypt's holy sites. To make the pilgrimage to holy Abydos was the early equivalent of making a Christian pilgrimage to Jerusalem or a Muslim pilgrimage to Mecca. There at Abydos we would see the bands of the faithful winding their way to the cemetery to set up their commemorative tablets. We would watch the white-robed body of some rich man disembarked from the barge that had brought it many weeks' journey from his home in order that, as his will has directed, it might be buried 'near the staircase of the great god at Abydos'.

12 The body of a rich man being brought to Abydos for burial

The site had long been hallowed, for here had existed those early prehistoric settlements of Amratians and Nagadans who, as we saw at the end of the last chapter, had laid the foundations of the realm of Upper Egypt. Abydos thus occupied a very special place in the sentiment and consciousness of the Egyptians. It was no wonder that some of the more remarkable sovereigns of the Middle and New Kingdoms should have constructed elaborate temples in the vicinity.

It is time to return to the ship; time to sail on. Once more we launch out on to the fast and friendly breast of the stream. On and on we sail, paddles pushing against the current. Past us slide the palm trees and mud huts, past us bob the inevitable cargo boats. There on the starboard bow we catch a glimpse of the ancient city of Coptos, which has waxed prosperous from prospecting for gold in the near-by desert, and from serving as a terminus for the Red Sea caravan trade. And then, 60 miles from Abydos, at last there hoves into view the renowned city which we have been longing to see. We have reached the heart and centre of Egypt. We have come to Thebes.

Homer, in the *Iliad*, called Thebes 'the Hundred-Gated', mistaking for city gates the square and soaring archways of her temples. The phrase does, however, convey something of the profound impression which the idea of the capital of imperial Egypt had made on the minds of the Greeks. Memphis, capital of Lower Egypt and second capital of the Two Lands, tended to be worldly and pleasure-loving. Not so Thebes. Thebes was new and busy. Her monuments and buildings had not been mellowed by time like those of the older city. Thebes was almost entirely the creation of a series of grandiose monarchs of the Middle, and more particularly of the New, Kingdoms, who desired to cut a splendid figure on the national and international stage. The city possessed the glittering sheen of many self-conscious and new-built capitals: Louis XIV's Versailles, Augustus the Strong's Dresden, or modern New Delhi and Brasilia. It was designed to impress: and impress it did.

As we step ashore from our ship, we would be overwhelmed by the scale and magnificence of the palaces and temples. At Thebes the princes of the Empire, ruling from Nubia to the river Euphrates, raised their boastful memorials to their own achievements. In the Middle Kingdom the formidable Mentu-hetep III built himself a temple at Deir el-Bahri, the cliff-sheltered recess on the western bank; and during the New Kingdom the female pharaoh Hatshepsut ordered her favourite

13 Deir el-Bahri: the Temple of Queen Hatshepsut, wife of Thutmose III, Eighteenth Dynasty, c. 1500 B.C.

courtier Senmut to build her a temple there that has always been considered one of the masterpieces of architecture(*13*). Amenophis III, Seti I and Ramses the Great all built themselves vast temple-palaces on this same bank, some of them of truly extraordinary dimensions. We Greek tourists would gape, for example, at the colossal statues which the long-dead king whom we would call Memnon (i.e. Amenophis III) had set up in front of his immense temple.

We would note, however, that even in august Thebes, as in all the other Egyptian towns which we have seen, the humbler folk have managed to set up house for themselves in the shadow of their betters. A sprawling city has sprung up round the temples and palaces. Yet even the presence of the heap of wooden or mud-brick hutments cannot detract from the stony splendour of the royal buildings that form its core. And away across the other side of the Nile we can discern the overwhelming outlines of those two stupendous edifices—the temples of Karnak(*27*) and Luxor.

If the sights of Thebes have not sated us, and we have the zest for further adventure, we can take ship once more to continue the voyage south. We have already travelled, in sailing from Busiris to Thebes, a distance of nearly 500 miles. Should we wish to make our way from Thebes to the most southerly town of the Empire, Napata, we shall have to travel 500 more. At Napata, a full 1,000 miles from the shores of the Mediterranean, the viceroys of the Egyptian pharaohs have raised, in the heart of Nubia, a Thebes in miniature. Ultimately, about 730 B.C., the native rulers of Nubia, thoroughly Egyptian in outlook in spite of their mingled negroid and bedouin blood, will march to the conquest of all Egypt under their grim leader Piankhi.

We shall find this second half of our journey exhausting. The first 100 miles of it will be uneventful. We will coast past Edfu, whose recently-built temple in the Greek style is an important shrine of Osiris; past Hierakonpolis, the earliest capital of Upper Egypt; and past its companion town Nekheb. We shall also be surprised by the easy-going appearance of the two distant townships of Syene (Aswan) and Elephantine, the original guardians of the wild frontier with Nubia. Elephantine, so called because it was the centre of the ivory trade in the form of elephant tusks, was a fortress picturesquely situated on an island in midstream; Aswan, its dependency, lay on the eastern bank, and was also engaged in the trade with the African interior that yielded a gaudy harvest of rare bird's feathers and animal skins. Both towns were wealthy and well endowed with temples.

The official frontier with Nubia had long ago been pushed far to the south, but these twin towns were still an important administrative and distributing centre. As soon as we leave them, however, we must face the perils of negotiating the First Cataract if we wish to see the famous temple at Abu Simbel (*18*): and by the time we have reached Napata we shall have traversed three cataracts in all. In point of fact, the later kings of the Ethiopian Kingdom of Napata, finally forsaking their cultural links with Egypt, had moved their capital a further 400 miles to the south, well below the Fifth Cataract, and even well below the junction of the Nile with the Atbara. At Meroe the Nubians had founded a provincial city, complete with brick pyramids, as extraordinary as their former capital of Napata. However, it is extremely unlikely that, even in the relatively

14 Nubians bearing tribute

stable epoch in which our group of Greek citizens is making its grand tour, we will want to penetrate as far south as Meroe. Indeed, it is probable that once we have reached Aswan we shall decide that the time has come to retrace our steps. We have no particular reason to plunge into the fiery furnace that is Nubia, with its sterile vistas of sand and granite. Let us instead return to take a closer look at some of the fascinating monuments which have already been visited—priding ourselves on the thought that we have, after all, traversed the whole length of the two vast kingdoms of Lower and Upper Egypt.

And what impression will we have gained? An impression of the deep blue river and the even more blue and deeper sky; of green plantations seamed with silvery canals; of brown bluffs studded with white huts and foursquare and dignified villas and temples. The land is peaceful and prosperous. Its peoples are busy and contented. It is a country unlike any other, unique and self-contained. Its resistance to change gave it its early strength and unity. Its resistance to change has sown the seeds of its fatal exhaustion and decay. But though the flower may perish, the lotus has borne a rich and brilliant blossom.

PYRAMIDS

To most of us, the most remarkable and puzzling of the monuments of ancient Egypt will always be its pyramids. They would certainly have been so to men like the little band of Greeks through whose eyes we have just taken a glance at the Nile valley. Indeed, it was probably some irreverent Greek who nicknamed these unique structures *pyramidia* or 'wheaten cakes', because they were shaped like the cakes that he was used to eating in Greece. And when our Greek saw them they were still in their pristine condition, sticking up out of the flat plain like so many mounds of whitest flour—white because many of them were cased with an outer skin of dazzling limestone that has long since been stripped away.

What can we say about them? How can we relate them to the daily life of the people who built them?

They were devoted, of course, to the burial of members of the royal family. In the earliest times the dead had merely been laid in a simple clay- or mat-lined pit in the sand: although even at this date the dead person was provided with the weapons,

15 Group of *mastaba* tombs at Sakkara. 16
(*right*) Sectional view of the interior of a *mastaba*,
showing mummy chamber 40–80 feet below hall
for offerings

clothing and food that he would require in
the next world. But if jackals were abroad,
or a sandstorm arose, the bodies of the
dead were liable to be exposed and dismembered; so the wealthier citizens decided
to provide themselves with more durable
sepulchres.

During the First Dynasty the kings and nobles began to construct the type of tomb which the modern Arabs term *mastabas*,
from their resemblance to the wooden bench which can often be
seen outside their houses. *Mastabas* were essentially dwelling-
houses built below the ground, topped with a white-
painted superstructure of mud brick containing a number of
store-rooms for the goods that were previously arranged
near the body. This superstructure was often elaborately
decorated.

During the two dynasties that followed, the corpse was not
placed in the subterranean rooms but in a chamber at the foot
of a deep central shaft, in the hope that the tomb-robbers would
be foiled when they came to try and loot the tomb. For the
profession of the tomb-robber, be it noted, is as time-honoured
as the profession of the undertaker.

In the subsequent dynasties of the Old Kingdom the *mastaba*
tomb still continued in fashion; but the bodies of the kings were
now confided to a completely novel type of tomb: the pyramid.
Essentially the pyramid, as we can see from a close study of the
important group of royal *mastabas* at Sakkara (*15*), was simply

the extension upwards of the flat-topped, sloping-sided super-structure of the *mastaba*. Around the king in his pyramid were disposed the *mastabas* of those who had served him in life, his queens, his sons and daughters, his officers of state, all enclosed in their separate tombs and arranged about their master in the manner of a complete miniature court.

The majority of the pyramids that we see today have a lonely and eroded appearance. They stand in battered isolation amid the choking drifts of the desert. Originally, however, they formed the centre-point of a highly elaborate network of dependent tombs and temples. The earliest, and in many ways the finest of them, was the so-called Step Pyramid which King Zoser, 'the Holy', founder of the Third Dynasty, built at Sakkara, south of Memphis(*17*). The Step Pyramid dates from about 2700 B.C. It was designed for the king by a man of undeniable genius, his vizier Imhotep. Imhotep, worshipped as a god by later genera-tions, was revered as the father of mathematics, medicine and architecture, and as the inventor of the calendar. He had the novel idea of placing a succession of *mastabas* on top of each other, like the tiers on a wedding cake, until he reached the total of six. The wedding-cake appearance was further heightened by a beautiful, glistening coating of fine limestone from the royal quarries at Tura. Deep under the pyramid was a wide shaft, at the bottom of which was a tomb chamber lined with pink granite and surrounded by a maze of subterranean passages; while above ground the towering structure was the focus of a network of outlying buildings. There were many temples, courts, halls and chapels, enclosed within a wall that was over a mile long. The wall, furnished with gateways and bastions, was copied from the celebrated 'White Wall' of Memphis, which had been built by the first Pharaoh, Narmer.

Like the Step Pyramid, all the other pyramids of the Old Kingdom were clustered together in the neighbourhood of Memphis, which for a thousand years was destined to be the capital of the Two Kingdoms. The pyramids lay on the west bank of the Nile, because it was behind the barrier of the western hills that the sacred boat of the sun sailed majestically into its nightly harbour. The architects first attempted to find a solid plateau of rock, situated as close as possible to the river, along which would later bump the rafts laden with blocks of

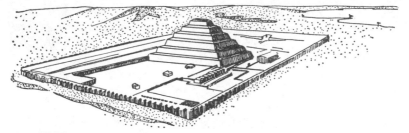

17 The Step Pyramid, Sakkara, built by King Zoser *c.* 2700 B.C.

stone from the quarries. Next the site was carefully surveyed with rods or cords, to align the corners of the projected pyramid on the four cardinal points of the compass. Then the chosen patch of rock was systematically cleared and levelled, the broken debris being systematically heaped up in the middle to form part of the core of the pyramid.

The Step Pyramid has the distinction of being the first great monument in the history of the world to be constructed of stone. More, it was a rare and delicate structure, possessed of a lightness and charm seldom achieved by Egyptian architects. There was an airy quality about it that was not to be repeated in the pyramids of the succeeding dynasties. It seems that Imhotep's masterpiece was neither severe nor symmetrical enough for the Pharaohs who occupied the throne after King Zoser. They desired a form of architecture that would mirror the increasingly rigid, centralised character of their method of government. Accordingly, they put in hand a series of piquant experiments concerning the form of the new style of royal sepulchre. The Layer Pyramid, the Unfinished Pyramid, the Pyramid of Meidum, the two Pyramids of Dahshur—all of them introduced variations that demonstrated the fascination which the pyramid idea exercised over the minds of Egypt's rulers.

The two Dahshur pyramids were almost certainly built by Snofru, first Pharaoh of the great Fourth Dynasty. And if the Pyramid of Meidum also belongs to Snofru, then that monarch built himself no less than three of these tremendous cenotaphs. The southern pyramid at Dahshur, called by archaeologists the Bent Pyramid, shows the individual features of its immediate predecessors. The northern pyramid, on the other hand, with its regularly sloping sides, leads us directly forward into the classic

42

18 The Temple of Ramses II at Abu Simbel, Nineteenth Dynasty: two of the
four colossal figures flanking the entrance

19 The smaller temple at Abu Simbel, Nineteenth Dynasty

20 The Sphinx and the Pyramid of Chephren, Giza, Fourth Dynasty

era of pyramid-building that begins with the reign of the next ruler, the renowned monarch known to history as Khufu, Khufwey, or—in the Greek—Cheops.

To Cheops belongs the Great Pyramid—loftiest of all, mightiest of the three huge pyramids that straddle the desert uplands at Giza. These three pyramids were justly considered by the ancients to be among the Wonders of the World. The Pyramid of Cheops was originally 490 feet high, and its base engulfs an area of no less than 31 acres—an area in which Westminster Abbey, St Paul's, and the cathedrals of Florence, Milan and St Peter's could comfortably be grouped. The Emperor Napoleon once sat down in its shadow and calculated, wistfully perhaps, that the mass of stone which it contained would serve to build a wall round France 10 feet high and one foot thick. The pyramid contains 2,300,000 blocks of stone, each averaging two and a half tons in weight. And these blocks were hoisted into position by means of palm-fibre ropes, wooden sledges, earthen ramps, and copper chisels(21). Yet these meagre tools were sufficient to enable the craftsmen who built it to work with extraordinary precision. They laid the red granite slabs of the outer casing so accurately that you could not put the blade of a knife between them. The gap between them is one ten-thousandth of an inch.

Here, in the large granite room at the core of the stone mountain, still reposes the sarcophagus of King Cheops: although the robbers have long ago done their unholy work. On one side of his man-made mountain the king had made provision for the squat, square *mastabas* of 64 of his relatives, ministers and courtiers; on the other side he built small pyramids for his three queens, flanked by eight double *mastabas* to house the remains of his favourite children.

A similar trinity of small pyramids was constructed around the near-by pyramid of King Mycerinus or Menkaura; and the third of the Pyramids of Giza, that of King Chephren or Khafra, is of additional interest because near one of its outer structures is situated the Great Sphinx(20). The Sphinx, once used by Turkish riflemen for target practice, is 240 feet long and 66 feet high. It was originally a knoll of rock, shaped by the royal artisans into a recumbent lion with a human head. It was probably coated with plaster and painted with gay colours, like

21 The building of the Great Pyramid of Cheops

most ancient Egyptian statues. The Greek word 'sphinx', by the way, may be derived from the Egyptian word meaning 'living image'; and between the paws of the fabulous beast once stood a statue of King Chephren.

The Pyramids of Giza, like the earlier pyramids, were surrounded by a regular series of buildings. Against the tapering cliff of their eastern face stood a stately temple; and from the temple a long stone causeway, over a mile long, sloped downhill towards a smaller temple in the valley. It was in this valley temple that the dead king lay, perhaps for many months, while the processes of embalming and purification were performed. Then he was taken in solemn procession along the causeway to be buried in his pyramid.

None of the later pyramids that were built during the next 13 or 14 centuries were as large as the Pyramids of Giza. Not only would it have been almost a physical impossibility to rival them, but the rulers who had inspired them had been men of unique power and prestige. Never again would the pharaohs of Egypt appear to their subjects to be quite so god-like and awe-inspiring as the pharaohs of the Fourth Dynasty. Beside their plain yet massive handiwork, the pyramids and sun-temples of the Fifth and Sixth Dynasties, extensive as they were, were almost garish and frivolous in comparison. True, the great kings Mentuhetep II of the Eleventh Dynasty and Amenemhat III of the Twelfth Dynasty built themselves grandiose pyramids. Amenemhat in particular took extraordinary precautions to foil the tomb robbers. His pyramid was honeycombed with false passages that led to dummy chambers: a kind of underground maze. His burial chamber, 22 feet long, was cut from a single block of yellow quartzite weighing 110 tons. But it was none the less becoming obvious that the pyramid method of burial provided no added protection for the precious corpses of their royal occupants. After the Middle Kingdom the pyramid went out of fashion for royal burials—although in the kingdom of Napata, far to the south, the Nubian kings were still being buried under pyramids 2,000 years later. Thereafter, the pharaohs of Egypt adopted the policy of hollowing out their tombs in the cliffs of the Valley of the Kings.

Why were the early rulers of Egypt so attracted by the idea of pyramid burial? How did the idea develop? It seems reasonable to suppose that the zig-zag outline of the first pyramids, resulting from piling up of *mastabas* on top of each other, gave birth to the notion that the pyramid was a kind of celestial step-ladder leading the dead king upward to his eternal home in the sky. An early text states bluntly that 'a staircase to heaven is laid for Pharaoh that he may ascend to heaven thereby'.

Later, when the steps were filled in and the sides of the pyramid became smooth, a second notion presented itself. The pyramid was then seen to resemble a holy stone, called the *benben*, which resided in a special shrine in the temple of the god Ra-Atum at Heliopolis. The *benben* probably represented the 'hillock of eternity' on which Ra-Atum, the creator of the world, had first made his appearance. Where better, then, could a dead king lie than inside a monument that brought to mind the 'hillock of eternity'? More, the *benben* and the pyramid were considered to be emblematic of the cone of the sun's rays as they flowed from heaven. Indeed, the *benben* at Heliopolis was probably gilded to resemble the shining cone of the sun as it poured down its life-giving rays upon the earth. So at the apex of every pyramid was placed a gilded pyramidion in the shape of the sacred *benben*.

We ought to mention, in passing, that the distinctive shape of the obelisk was also derived from the *benben*. In the case of the obelisk, however, the little gilded pyramidion was placed at the summit of an immensely tall granite pillar. The tapering sides of the pillar could then be used to recall the achievements of the pharaoh who caused it to be erected. In Britain, of course, there is a fine obelisk in 'Cleopatra's Needle', which soars between the trees that line the Thames Embankment. Actually, the Needle does not belong to the reign of Cleopatra at all, but dates from the reign of the Napoleon of Egypt, Tuthmosis III, who ruled 1,400 years earlier.

22 Obelisk at Karnak

Obelisks were often erected in pairs, and the twin of 'Cleopatra's Needle' now stands in Central Park in New York. Among other obelisks, we might mention the two impressive pairs which Queen Hatshepsut of the Eighteenth Dynasty raised in her temple at Deir el-Bahri. One of the four still survives, and is almost 100 feet in height. The tallest surviving obelisk of all, however, is the column from Karnak, no less than 105 feet high, dating from the reign of Tuthmosis III, that stands outside the church of St John Lateran in Rome. Obelisks, being portable, have proved to be of particular interest to foreign plunderers. Other capitals beside New York and Rome have adorned themselves with obelisks. The companion to the Karnak obelisk at Rome now stands at Constantinople, and in the Place de la Concorde in Paris is one of a pair of obelisks from Abu Simbel.

48

The pyramid, then, was once the central point of a special township, most of which has now disappeared. Just as the king had once dwelt in his palace, surrounded by his family and his courtiers, so now he lay in his palace of eternity, surrounded by those same relatives and courtiers. The pyramid-city was a city of the dead. But in this dead city a host of living men still walked, for the king and his noblemen had left behind them substantial sums to engage priests to pray for their souls, to hire guards to protect their bones, and workmen to maintain their sepulchres in good repair. Sometimes whole cities, as at Lahûn, were built to house the workmen and officials who many hundreds of years later would still be keeping alive the cult of the dead pharaoh. By this means, the kings of Egypt ensured that, for long centuries after they had passed from the warm sunlight into the gloomy shade, the necropolis would re-echo with the chanting of hymns and the tread of the sentries.

We must understand that these elaborate arrangements were not undertaken solely to flatter the vanity or allay the fears of the dead ruler. The ordinary folk of Egypt had a vested interest in keeping alive the memory of their ancient kings. The spiritual influence of a good pharaoh continued to shed benefit on his people after his death. By keeping his cult vigorous, by worshipping him daily, his powers of intercession with his fellow gods on behalf of his former people were renewed. The king was as valuable an asset to his subjects when he was a dead god as when he had been a living one; he continued to be a source of psychic power. That was why the Egyptians buried their pharaohs with such loving care in such fantastic tombs as the pyramids—and why they were always dismayed and heartbroken when those tombs were violated by desperate and blasphemous hands.

A VISIT TO A TEMPLE

Unless they were employed there as craftsmen or artists, the ordinary folk of ancient Egypt would have little cause to visit the pyramid-cities.

It was not among the tombs that the people of Egypt chiefly delighted to honour their kings and gods, but in the temples and palaces. In many instances the two kinds of building, as in the case of the immense palace-temple of Ramses II at Medinet

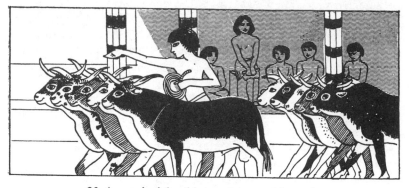

23 A provincial nobleman inspects his cattle

Habu, were interchangeable. Was not the king himself a god, the living incarnation of Horus? Then what was more natural than that his temple should be his palace and his palace his temple? The king's life, after all, was a continuous sacrament.

The presence of pharaoh was a daily reality in every temple throughout the Two Lands. It was the daily rite which he performed with his own hands that made effective the rites that were performed simultaneously in every temple throughout his kingdom. For this and other reasons, the temple was the irresistible magnet which drew to itself every man, woman and child in the local community. However small and isolated the temple might be, however obscure and unpretentious the god or goddess to whom it was dedicated, it was the very hub of their lives. This was because the temple was not only a spiritual and social centre but an economic centre as well. The temple performed the same role in ancient Egypt as the cathedral in mediaeval Europe. It was the dual source of cultural inspiration and physical employment. As in mediaeval Europe, with the exception of the estates of the feudal barons almost the entire ownership of land and property was concentrated in the hands of the king and his chief priests. In theory, the king held the Black Land in trusteeship for his fellow gods. His chief priests were therefore his principal tenants, although they gradually became more or less the unchallenged rulers of their own domains—in the way that the Abbot of Tintern or Rievaulx would carry out his ecclesiastical duties while superintending the agriculture, stock-breeding and building-work throughout his wide province(23). The main temples acted not only as the distributors of their own bounty, but of the royal bounty too. An entire population of civil servants, scribes, policemen, craftsmen, artisans and artists was fed and clothed from the priestly granaries and storerooms. The chief priests collected taxes on behalf of the king and doled out rewards and necessities as they saw fit. They were thus the instruments and regulators of the state economy and wielded enormous power.

Like the mediaeval cathedrals of Europe, the more massive temples of Egypt were also subject to a process of architectural addition and subtraction that lasted many centuries. In the prehistoric or predynastic epoch a certain spot would be considered hallowed; in the Old or Middle Kingdoms a modest wooden or sandstone kiosk would be erected there; and by the time of the New Kingdom or the Ptolemies, as likely as not the simple kiosk would have been transformed into a vast and rambling edifice spread out over an area of 400–500 acres. The impression which the ruins of these great temples makes on the modern visitor is one of inhuman regularity and severity: but at the height of their glory, when their walls were painted with glowing colours, when their flagpoles were gay with bunting, when their courts were enlivened with the flamboyant vestments of their priests, they presented an appearance of teeming variety and complexity.

Let us return for a moment to the past and rejoin that party of Greek explorers who are travelling in the Black Land towards the close of its splendid day.

We have decided to spend the afternoon examining the glories of Karnak, the most magnificent of Egyptian religious sites. The previous three or four days, armed with a pass from a high government official, we have been making a thorough inspection of the wonders of Thebes. We have marvelled at the remains of the Malkata Palace of Amenophis III and at his Colossi of Memnon. We have stared at the gross and glowering Ramesseum and the palace-temple of Medinet Habu, pride of the *parvenu* dynasty of the Ramessides. We have spent a whole day admiring Queen Hatshepsut's temple at Deir el-Bahri(13). Now we have crossed to the eastern bank of the river, where we have just been

24 A temple pylon

revelling in the architectural beauties of the temple of Luxor. Luxor is a smaller appendage of Karnak, mainly constructed in a later and more consistent style during the reign of Amenophis III, that urbane pharaoh whose name we hear so often in our travels. We shall see no single feature at Karnak that will rival the peerless terraces of Deir el-Bahri or the papyrus colonnades of Luxor; yet Karnak, purely in point of size, is the largest religious site that the world has ever seen. (Though further north, at Hawara in the Fayûm, our Greek friends allege that they have been allowed to view a pyramid-temple built by Ammenemes III of the Twelfth Dynasty that dwarfs even Karnak itself. This is the famous Labyrinth, described by Herodotus, that is nowadays a shapeless sprawl of rubble.)

Behold us, then, on our pilgrimage to Karnak. Thoughtful, silent, slightly footsore, a little irked by the remorseless energy of our leader—small, dapper, bossy, dogmatic—we have emerged from the temple and are now walking along the mile-long avenue that links Luxor with Karnak. This avenue, 80 feet wide, is flanked on each side by ram-headed sphinxes. The route is lined with a motley collection of tiny shrines and tabernacles; and when we are half-way along it we glance to our right to see the coppery sunshine gleaming on the sickle-shaped lake called Asheru, standing beside a large subsidiary temple sacred to the vulture goddess Mut, consort of Amon-Ra and Ruler of Karnak. Against the walls of her temple stand many statues representing her formidable friend, the lion goddess Sekhmet, patroness of the powers of chaos.

As we near the end of this unique avenue, constructed by Amenophis III for his ceremonial processions, we can see looming up before us the first of Karnak's ten pylons(24). Pylons are those twin towers with a double gateway between them which are such a distinctive feature of Egyptian architecture. Beyond the first pylon we can discern no less than three more before the avenue that sweeps straight between them finally comes to a

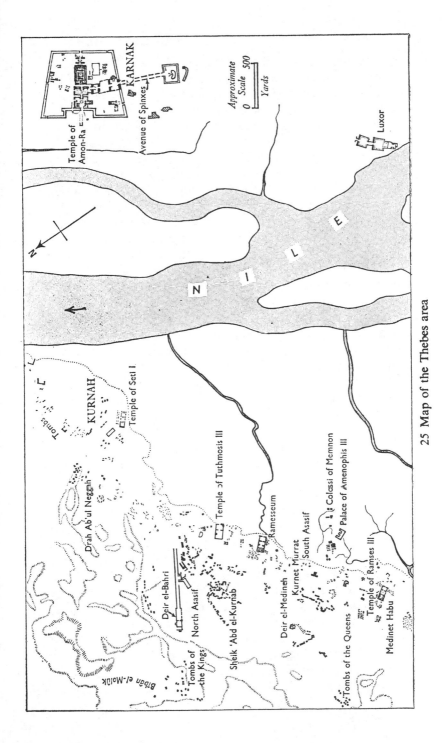

25 Map of the Thebes area

stop against the southern door of the temple itself. The prospect of leaving the broiling sunshine for the dim, cool interior of the temple is inviting. Yet we must postpone this pleasant experience for another ten minutes, because our indefatigable leader is suggesting that, instead of making our entrance through the southern doorway, we should turn sharp left and skirt the outer wall until we come to the western entrance. We have to admit that he has a good reason for submitting us to this inconvenience; in this way we shall better appreciate how Egyptian temples are laid out. Grumbling a little, notwithstanding, we head for the western entrance; and as we walk we catch sight over the top of the stone wall of the temple of Khonsu, fitting snugly into one corner of the temple compound. The young warrior Khonsu, son of Mut and Amon-Ra, is the third member of the heavenly trinity which is worshipped at Karnak.

And now at last we are ready to step beneath the huge western pylon into the temple of Amon-Ra, King of the Gods. Like many of the other principal temples of Egypt, Karnak is orientated on an east–west axis. The worshipper thus stands with his face to the east, just as he does, coincidentally, in Christian churches. As the sun rises above the eastern horizon it will symbolise the youthful Horus Harakhte. Gradually it will soar above the mid-point of the east–west pylons, one tower of which represents Horus's mother Isis and the other Isis's inseparable companion, the goddess Nephthys. And as it sinks towards the west, it will neatly bisect the temple, with that effect of symmetry so dear to the hearts of Egyptians.

Now, at the moment when we are about to enter the outer courtyard, it is noon and the sun stands directly overhead. The sweat pours down our faces after our long trek from Luxor. At this time of day the sun ceases to personify the young Horus, and is held to assume its full maturity in the form of the god Ra. This bewildering throng of gods and goddesses, most of whom seem to be quick-change artists, is, of course, much less strange to a party of ancient Greeks than it is to a modern reader. Horus, for example, is the actual forerunner of the Greek Apollo, so it is little wonder that a Greek would feel at ease in the vast, sun-warmed edifice of Karnak. To a Greek, a visit to Karnak is only a little more unfamiliar than a visit to the Orthodox Cathedral in Moscow would be to a devout Anglican.

Ancient Greeks would be perfectly accustomed to the company of the gods playing a divine version of musical chairs.

With a quickening of the pulse, we walk towards the immense outer pylon. From its crest rise six slender flagpoles, gilded and fixed in sturdy clamps, and from the flagpoles long narrow banners painted with sacred emblems droop limply in the heat.

We step through the black wedge of shadow and find ourselves in the spacious outer courtyard. This is the recent portion of the temple—the equivalent of the Victorian additions to mediaeval churches. The

26 Girls carrying temple offerings

outer pylon itself was built as recently as the Ptolemaic era, while the beautiful colonnaded courtyard in which our exacting leader has permitted us a short halt was also built in the late era by Shashank I. Shashank, who founded the Twenty-second Dynasty, was an energetic soldier of foreign descent with a generous dash of Libyan blood in his veins. Like most other conquerors of Egypt, with the exception of certain brutish leaders of the Assyrians and the Persians, Shashank and his forbears had fallen under the spell of the people whom they had conquered and made obeisance to their genial gods.

The courtyard is filled with people hurrying hither and thither. In this ante-chamber of Amon-Ra, where the public sections of the liturgy are performed every day, no face betrays any sign of fear or restraint. Plainly to serve the great god is a joyful thing. Four pretty girls, their wrists and ankles jingling with bangles, are walking towards a small temple whose façade juts from the wall on our right. On their heads they balance plaited baskets containing offerings for the altars within. We can distinguish conical loaves of bread, the dangling dead heads of waterfowl, the crisp leaves of green vegetables. To our left, an elderly sculptor and his young apprentice are perched aloft on a wooden scaffolding, effecting leisurely repairs to a portion of the frieze that runs round a small shrine. The slow tap of their mallets and copper chisels floats drowsily on the shimmering, heat-dazed air. A few yards further away, on a bench within the discreet shelter of an arcade, two dignified old gentlemen in flowing robes have anticipated the siesta hour by snatching a quiet snooze. And now, chattering and laughing, a straggling crocodile of schoolboys in short tunics emerges from the gateway of the second pylon on the other side of the courtyard. They carry with them their writing-blocks and pen-cases. Three or four of them slap and punch each other, fooling about in the relief of being released from lessons. The stoop-shouldered and harrassed-looking scribe in charge of them, his temper inflamed by a long session with them in the class-room, aims an ineffectual cuff or two at the ears of the nearest pair of offenders.

As we continue to stand and get our breath back, a short, stout man wrapped in a voluminous garment of purple enters in stately fashion through the gateway behind us. He marches across the courtyard, flourishing his long, gold-bound staff, a brace of secretaries fawning and fluttering behind him. He is dark-featured, bearded, hook-nosed, his complexion swarthy. Could he be some visiting diplomat, or perhaps the chief magistrate of some distant Egyptian province? We see him step aside to bow gravely to a pair of shaven-headed priests who have emerged from the cloistered walk on the left. The skirts of their white robes are folded across their left arms, and on their chests, suspended from golden chains, hang the square plaques or pectorals which are the badge of high office. The jewels and brilliant enamelling of the pectorals splinter the sunlight into a thousand rays as the two priests interrupt their solemn discourse and turn to acknowledge the salute of the purple-clad official. Our small group too they favour with a dignified nod, before passing through the first pylon into the secular world beyond the enclosure wall. They are much too preoccupied, or much too imbued with the exquisite politeness of their ancient civilisation, to express any surprise at our outlandish garb and uncouth demeanour.

Now, at last, our leader allows us to forsake the heat and dust of high noon for the interior of the building. We move forward and present our papyrus passes to the alert, courteous temple guard on duty at the door. Then we step beneath the second pylon, the handiwork of the professional soldier Horemhab, who carried out a great deal of work at Karnak. Then we are in the famous hypostyle hall. The sheer scale of it takes our breath away as effectively as the sudden chill that pierces us to the marrow. In this hall, as we

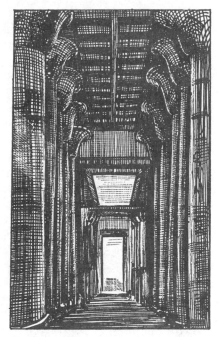

27 The hypostyle hall of the Temple of Amon-Ra at Karnak

can see from the carvings and frescoes about us, some of the most important royal rituals are celebrated.

Our first impression is of being crushed by a suffocating mass of painted stone. Craning our heads back, we can see the light filtering down through the clerestory windows 80 feet above us. We begin to walk down the central aisle. On either hand soar a line of bulbous columns, monstrously thick, their tops decorated with capitals representing papyrus buds. The petals of these buds are open. And beyond these two inner lines are other, slimmer columns, rank upon rank of them.

If we were to count, we would find that there were 12 of the immensely thick inner columns and 60 of the more slender outer ones. The papyrus-buds that crown the latter are not open but closed. Once again, we are presented with an example of the symbolism so dear to the Egyptians. The taller inner columns reach closer to the sun as it travels over the temple, and its noonday warmth is supposed to have induced them to open. Every single one of these columns, large and small shimmers with painted scenes that cover every inch of them from floor to ceiling. For some minutes we dumbly and dutifully study the gods, kings and ceremonies depicted on them, circling the columns in order to follow the sequence of scenes to their close.

With a sneaking sense of shame, we are ultimately driven to admit to ourselves that, from the architectural point of view, this amazing structure is not truly in the highest class. It is too cramped, too gloomy and oppressive. In fact, the Egyptians do not appear to have been as good at planning their interiors as they were at planning their exteriors. Yet it is impossible not to be overwhelmed by a lofty, echoing hall which is 190 feet long and 338 feet wide. It is certainly a fitting monument to the two dynamic pharaohs of the Twenty-third Dynasty who built it: Seti I and his successor, the great Ramses II, who reigned for over 60 years. These men typified the coarsened, over-assertive tastes of an Egypt which fancied itself to be at its zenith, but which was actually past its peak. Yet whether it was past its peak or not, the great hall at Karnak could only be the product of a still mighty and still remarkable country.

It is therefore with somewhat mixed feelings that we leave the hypostyle hall: to be struck once more by the blistering heat of the sun the moment we emerge into the inner courtyard. We have just passed beneath the third pylon in this west–east axis, a pylon of exceptional height, surmounted by no fewer than eight flagpoles from which hang an assortment of coloured streamers. This gateway is the handiwork of the omnipresent Amenophis III; and to provide materials for its construction he had no hesitation in tearing down a pretty little pavilion of Sesostris I that dated from the Twelfth Dynasty. He then utilised the blocks in the foundations of his own pylon. This was, you may say, reprehensible and even sacrilegious conduct: but the truth is that the majority of pharaohs showed no compunction whatever in destroying the monuments of their predecessors in order to raise grander ones to themselves. It was not merely the temples that suffered this regal plundering: it occurred in palaces and—yes—even in tombs. And where the monuments of ancestors or rivals could not be actually torn down, they were coolly appropriated by means of chiselling out

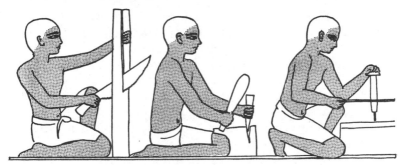

28 Carpenters at work in the temple

the name and titles of their original owner and substituting those of the imperial thief. Not a proceeding worthy of great kings: but it is commonplace that great kings often show great failings.

In this inner courtyard we pause for a moment to adjust our eyes to the sunlight, blinking up at the enormous obelisks of Tuthmosis I that dwarf the courtyard. The walls are crowded with the more-than-lifesize statues of former notabilities. These groups of statues are a common feature of temple courtyards. At the foot of a colossal statue of Amenophis III stands the effigy of one of his devoted servants, Amenhotep, son of Hapu (our omniscient leader is good enough to translate the hiero-glyphic names for us). The statues of a score of other fortunate officials, all of them painted in the usual lifelike colours, have also found a niche here, in the presence of their former masters and within the precinct of the King of the Gods. There they will dwell for ever, in the house of Amon-Ra, wearing their decora-tions and tokens of honour, their vivid eyes staring out con-fidently into eternity.

Turning, we can see behind us a forest of wooden planks, covering the whole of one wall. On the planks, a throng of cheerful stonemasons are busy stripping the courses of the wall in order to rebuild it anew. With such ever-present gangs con-tinually rending the air with their laughter and the clatter of their tools, it is no wonder that Egyptian temples are not the abodes of austere silence which we had imagined them to be. From dawn to dusk, day in and day out, the task of remodelling or enlarging the structure of the temple is carried on. After all, these workmen are the staff of the temple itself, part of the

59

temple family, so it is only policy to keep them actively employed. As we saw, the temples are centres of economic life, and at one of the periodical censuses, taken in the reign of Ramses III, it was discovered that these two great temples of Thebes possessed a total of 90,000 workmen, 500,000 head of cattle, 400 orchards, 80 ships and 50 workshops. They drew their revenues from tithes and taxes levied on 65 of the most prosperous townships in Egypt and the Egyptian empire in Palestine.

Look. If you glance out there to the left, you can see through the gate a sun-drenched landscape alive with men sowing, ploughing, digging canals, tending crops and groves. All these peasants and the earth which they tend is the property of Amon-Ra. And it is the duty of Amon-Ra's high priests to maintain them. In similar fashion during the Old Kingdom, when the priests were not yet so powerful and the king was still the chief source of state patronage, the building of the pyramids had played a similar economic role. It is customary to represent the pyramid-builders of the Fourth Dynasty as cruel tyrants who herded their subjects together into abject slave-gangs. Moaning and panting, their backs striped by the lash of their overseers, they are pictured hauling on the sledges that hold the great blocks of stone. This image is almost certainly false. Subtle engineering as much as brute strength played its part in the building of the pyramids, and a large proportion of the labour force must have consisted of workmen of a high degree of training and accomplishment. These men were not helots but skilled men who rejoiced in their abilities. The pyramids of Giza are scarcely the emblem of a soulless tyranny, for the Egyptians of that era were only too eager to prove in this way their devotion to their kings, whose divine authority held the state together and gave it a prosperity without parallel in the ancient world.

Raising the pyramids was not only a sign of love and respect —it also provided plenty of jobs and pay. For three whole months in each year the Black Land lay beneath the waters of the Nile, and every effort had to be made to slow down the rate of subsidence in order to conserve the precious floods for as long as possible. What was the poor peasant to do during this annual period of the Inundation? Was he simply to cower in his hut and stare helplessly at the sheet of water outside his door? No—his king had provided him with the means of earning his daily bread throughout the weeks which otherwise would have been unproductive and monotonous. He enrolled himself in the royal labour force and went to work at Giza. Fortunately this was the best, indeed the only time of the year when the blocks on their wooden rafts could be floated right on to the rocky plateau and right on to the site where the work was being carried on(21). The task that the peasant performed at Giza made him feel that he was contributing towards the continued prosperity of the land in which he lived. For to take loving care of the embalmed remains of the king by providing it with a fitting sepulchre was, as we have seen, to ensure that the king's beneficent influence would continue to exert itself within the bounds of his former kingdom.

Four and a half thousand years later, when the Suez Canal was built, the system was still functioning, but in a thoroughly degraded manner. The Turkish pashas were not the enlightened rulers that the native pharaohs had been, and the wretched men in their gangs were, in fact, literally slaves. It may have been the sight of the Turkish labour gangs that confirmed the European Egyptologists of a century ago in their belief that the pharaohs of the Fourth Dynasty were tyrants of the same stamp. Of course, the Greeks with whom we are taking our imaginary journey are not at all shocked by the idea of slavery. The peculiar institution of slave-owning was fundamental to Greek civilisation. Slavery in Egypt, on the other hand, was a minor and haphazard affair, and slaves were never numerous. Moreover they were almost without exception foreign captives. Freeborn Egyptians were seldom sold into slavery; and since it was certainly free-born Egyptians who must have built the pyramids, few of them—*ex hypothesi*—can have been slaves.

But now our leader is turning with his usual brisk and businesslike air towards the pylon ahead of us: and when he begins to stalk forward we meekly file after him. He is a man who knows his own mind. The façade of this particular pylon, we notice, is even more of a mixture of styles than the ones we have already seen. We are looking, in fact, at the other portion of the temple, or roughly the eastern half of it. Before the wilful Tuthmosides began to 'improve' it, during the opening years of the New Kingdom, it was an open, rather primitive structure. Now it looks like a coral reef in a particularly busy corner of the Indian Ocean. Still another pylon has been tacked on to the original façade, imprisoning the red basalt obelisks of Queen Hatshepsut whose gleaming copper-sheathed tips stick up into the azure sky behind the pylon with an undeniably ill-judged effect. So many architectural bits and pieces have been piled up, one on top of the other, that all sense of the original scale and harmony has been lost. The outermost region of the inner temple through which we are now picking our way is little more than a bizarre jumble of granite, basalt, limestone and painted plaster. True, the symmetry so vital to Egyptian tastes has been preserved, but it has degenerated into a crowded, mad kind of symmetry. It is almost as though one has strolled into a sort of religious super-market. A dozen pharaohs have vied with each other in making costly additions to this, the heart of the temple, and in doing so they have not hesitated to tear down the pious and loving handiwork of earlier kings. The temple labour force, and particularly that portion of it which concerns itself with the decorative arts, has here been working overtime. Every square inch of walls, pillars and ceilings have been covered with carvings and paintings. Our Greek companions, accustomed to a more chaste conception of architecture, turn up their noses at this finicky display; and we must admit that we ourselves have not been favourably impressed by this garish exhibition, so different from everything we have previously seen in the harmonious and unified surroundings of Deir el-Bahri and Luxor. Yet this, after all, is how the ancient Egyptians actually prefer the majority of their temples to look. And who are we, with the interiors of most of our cathedrals strewn and studded with lady-chapels, crusaders' tombs, commemorative plaques, marble effigies of bishops and merchants, and rusty iron stoves—who are we to criticise them?

There is yet a third courtyard to be traversed before we plunge once again into the grateful coolness of the interior of the temple. We are now in the sixth and last section of the sacred structure. It is extremely dark here. We are approaching the innermost shrine, the holy of holies; the atmosphere is close and oppressive. The apertures in the clerestory are unusually small, and we are half stifled by the smoke and fume of fitfully burning torches and by the stench of some potent, musky incense. Gingerly we pick our way forward past the projecting cornices of painted stone, avoiding the kneeling or recumbent forms of priests and devotees. Someone is chanting a hymn to the sun in a soft and high-pitched tone.

There is nothing accidental about the veiled and shrouded character of this portion of the temple. Indeed the blackness increases with every step we take. It is as the result of a deliberate plan, here as elsewhere, that the visitor is led through a series of wide and noisy courtyards into narrow and silent ones, through well-lit halls into ones that are increasingly murky. In this way his senses have been gradually conditioned as he nears the end of his pilgrimage, and when he finally reaches the tabernacle of the god he is in a subdued and reverent frame of mind.

At last we have reached the point where we can raise our eyes to the niche in which resides the most hallowed of the thousand statues of Karnak—the statue of Amon-Ra, patron of Thebes and the Theban monarchs who have raised Egypt to the pinnacle of her glory. Truly the house-god of such puissant pharaohs merits the title of King of Kings(29).

A glimpse of gold and enamels and precious stones. An impression of a golden face staring through the clouds of incense with an expression of tranquil majesty. We make a deep obeisance. Then we turn and withdraw from the sanctuary, shuffling slowly backwards in the way in which we have seen the local worshippers make their exit.

Our visit to Karnak is over.

Even the leader of our little party, fervid partisan of everything Athenian though he is, has been impressed by the grandeur and lavishness of what he has just seen. The Egyptians are a rich and a generous race—but nowhere are they so prodigal as in the way in which they do

29 Amon-Ra

honour to their gods. And the gods of Egypt are wealthy gods and know how to repay such faithful devotion. They have been kind to the people who dwell in their valley.

Leaving the temple through a small side gateway in the middle courtyard, we wander towards the wide square lake that stands beside the older part of the temple. Many temples possess sacred lakes of this kind, complete with stone quays and flights of steps dipping down into the water. The lakes play a leading role in many of the temple rituals; and on the margin of the lake at Karnak we see, resting in its alabaster cradle, the wooden boat which is a replica of the boat in which the god Ra sails daily across the heavens. It is carried in processions and is part of the basic equipment of every Egyptian temple(*83*). As we touch its gold-encrusted timbers, we reflect that this religion, absurdly complicated and childish as it seems, is deeply and sincerely cherished by the Egyptians themselves. The reflection makes us feel rather humble. Can there perhaps be more to the cult of these unfamiliar gods than we, in our superior way, would like to suppose. . . ?

It is refreshing to loiter for a moment beneath the metallic fronds of the palm-trees. There is even the hint of a breeze. The orb of the sun rests motionless on the unruffled surface of the lake. Behind us the enclosure wall of the temple runs straight and smooth and white. Both wall and temple look so solid that it is hard to believe that presently the potency of Amon-Ra and his divine company must dwindle and their temples decay. Yet posterity will be left in no doubt whatever that the builders of the Theban temples were a capable and noble race of men.

HOUSES

We have, first of all, considered the pyramids and temples of ancient Egypt, and it would have been impossible not to have accorded them their rightful place at the beginning of our account of Egyptian architecture.

We are now free to turn our attention to less weighty matters, and to look at the actual houses in which the ancient Egyptians passed their daily lives. We must bear in mind, however, that these houses were modelled on the royal and religious buildings that had set the basic standards of craftsmanship and design. It was the techniques which were first tried out in the *mastaba* tombs of the early dynasties that led directly to the forms of domestic architecture. Furthermore, we have seen that there was a special sense in which the palaces and temples influenced the daily life of the great mass of the people. It was as though the economic and artistic fortunes of the population of London were to be largely controlled by Buckingham Palace, Hampton Court, Westminster Abbey and St Paul's. In all walks of life it was the king and his priests—and the king himself was the chief priest—who set the fashion. Thus the houses of the leading courtiers were copied from the palaces of the kings, and the houses of the provincial nobility and landed gentry were copied in turn from those of the leading courtiers.

The Egyptians began to perfect their building methods and materials at an astonishingly early date, perhaps under the influence of certain ideas of Mesopotamian origin. At the outset of Egyptian history, before 3000 B.C., Egyptian builders had already devised a general-purpose mud brick of a standard size, and were making a smaller type of brick for decorative work (*30*). These bricks were reinforced by an admixture of chopped straw, or of sand when straw was not available. They certainly knew how to fire in the kiln red bricks of our own type; but as Professor Emery, the excavator of the Sakkara tombs, has commented, for the most part they were 'satisfied with their sun-dried brick, and in this they were right, for even today, after 5,000 years, these bricks show a hardness almost equal to a soft stone' (*Archaic Egypt*, p. 180).

The alluvial mud of the Nile was put to a host of other uses. It was a magnificent all-round material. On occasion it was compounded with strips of linen, rather as modern concrete can

30 Builders at work

be pre-stressed with steel rods, and the resulting long hard blocks were used for beams and lintels. The early builders also bonded their bricks in fancy patterns to secure elaborately recessed façades, and employed lengths of reed matting or layers of thin sticks at every half-dozen courses to bind the wall together.

The same materials were used to construct roofs and ceilings. For the roof, the area to be covered was first spanned by lengths of timber, either rounded or neatly squared off; then matting was laid on these rafters, and the whole topped by a thick slab of mud plaster. If a painted ceiling was required, another expanse of matting was stretched on battens beneath the rafters and given a thin coating of plaster to provide a ground for the artist. Floors were made of mud plaster covered with a bone-hard layer of gypsum. The Nile, which already provided the ancient Egyptians with most of the necessities of life, thus also provided them with the principal ingredients of their dwelling places. No wonder, then, that they lavished so much attention on the cult of Haapi, the god of their river.

There are few remains or representations of houses to show us exactly how Egyptians lived at the outset of their long history. But as the *mastaba* tombs were 'houses of the dead', the twin version of 'houses of the living', it is not difficult to deduce what the royal palaces, at least, must have looked like. Presumably the only real difference between a house of the dead and a house of the living was that the former was built below instead of above ground. The disposition and contents of the store-rooms, granaries and private apartments must have been generally the same in both cases. With the coming of the Middle Kingdom, however, our knowledge of the domestic aspects of Egyptian civilisation becomes much more substantial. There are not only finely painted and sculptured tombs at such places as Deir el-Bersheh, Beni Hasan, Meir and Qaw el-Kebir, but a little chamber in the tomb of the Chancellor Meketra at Deir el-Bahri yielded a wonderful series of wooden models which give us a unique glimpse into the architecture and the day-to-day life of the epoch. At Lahûn or Kahûn, in the Fayûm area of Lower Egypt, the great Egyptologist Sir Flinders Petrie excavated a large walled township that once housed the workmen who built the pyramid-town of King Sesostris I, and the priests and officials who later maintained his cult there. Here there were large houses for the important residents, including what appears to have been a private residence for the king himself, and blocks of small dwellings for the workers that remind one startlingly of our modern housing

31 A workman's house

development (*31*). Other sites of the Middle Kingdom, in particular the fortresses, such as the one on Uronarti Island just above the Second Cataract, also reveal what a firm grasp the Egyptians possessed of the 'council house' type of architecture.

When we come down to New Kingdom times, we are afforded an even more impressive example of this municipal style of architecture in the workmen's quarter at Tel el-Amarna. The quarter was carefully laid out according to a clear-cut grid system. At Tel el-Amarna, where the fanatic king Akhenaton built himself a brand new capital, we also possess a remarkably complete picture of a royal palace and its surroundings. Here we can see the king's apartments, with its two harems and its hypostyle hall; and on the other side of the 'Royal Road' that fronts the palace are the great and small temples, the barracks and military quarters, the clerks' offices and storehouses that occupy the central portion of the capital. If we add to the knowledge which we have gained from Tel el-Amarna the knowledge derived from other Eighteenth Dynasty palaces and their precincts, such as the two palaces at Deir el-Ballas and the immense multiple palace of Akhenaton's father Amenophis III at Thebes, then we can safely claim to possess a more or

67

less all-inclusive impression of the domestic repertoire of the New Kingdom architect.

In the previous section we took a look at a representative temple, built when the wealth and good fortune of Egyptian civilisation were at their peak. Let us take a similar look at an Egyptian house of the same epoch. We shall inspect the villa of a well-to-do citizen of the Eighteenth Dynasty, the kind of villa which would incorporate many of the features of royal palaces on the one hand, and most of those of humbler dwellings on the other. From the point of view of design and construction it will be typical of the houses of the whole dynastic epoch—for in a country where the conservative habit of mind was innate, where technical innovation was rare, and where the range of raw materials remained constant from one generation to the next, one would not often expect to stumble on a mansion of revolutionary aspect.

Our villa could be situated either in the countryside—among, say, the bird-haunted marshes of the Delta—or in the prosperous upper-class suburbs of Thebes or Memphis. The rule in the cities of ancient Egypt was the same as that in the cities of the modern world: the poor were huddled together in cramped and over-crowded conditions, while the wealthy occupied choice and self-contained houses that stand in their own well-kept gardens, surrounded by leafy palms and protected by high walls.

The walls of the surrounding villas are plain and square, but we note that the wall of the one which we are now to visit has a prettily scalloped top to it. There is

32 The garden of a country villa

68

33 A villa

only one entrance into the compound: stout double doors set in a charming gateway shaped like a miniature pylon. The wooden doors are opened for us as we approach by two of the estate workmen.

We are immediately struck by the 'contemporary' appearance of the house and its setting. We catch sight of it through an arching pergola with climbing plants trained across its latticed timbers. On our right is a square pool sprinkled with fat pink water-lilies, on whose waxen fronds butterflies are sunning themselves; and on our left are neatly dug flower and vegetable beds. If it was not for the palm trees, the garden has the appearance of a well-tended country garden on a July afternoon in the south of England(32).

The house itself has the straight lines and 'functional' air of a modern building(33). In deference to local conditions, however, there are no windows, only grilles set high up in the walls. The fact that it is a wide, one-storey building with a slightly raised centre section that serves as a roof garden heightens the impression that it is the kind of villa that Mies van der Rohe, Gropius or Maxwell Fry might have devised for a wealthy client. It is a large, dignified house, completely square in plan, with a frontage of approximately 100 feet. We calculate that it could easily contain 25–30 rooms.

When we come nearer, we can see that it stands on a kind of

69

solid brick platform; the front door is four to five feet above ground level, and is reached by means of a gently inclined ramp. The ramp leads us to a small projecting vestibule, though which we see the inside of the house. On entering, we find ourselves in a spacious oblong hall, embellished with a double row of columns. This is the hall in which guests and visitors gather before moving into the inner apartment. The columns are of wood, and stand on round stone bases. Wood is a scarce commodity in Egypt, a land in which trees are scanty, and to which cedars of Lebanon were floated down from Byblos in the time of the Second Dynasty, and probably even earlier. Much of the wood which we shall see in the villa, whether used for the columns or elsewhere, is actually a veneer or facing covering the prosaic mud-brick beneath. Wood and stone were very scarce materials, rendered even more so by the cost and difficulty of transport. It is therefore not surprising that, when an Egyptian moved house, or built himself another one, he packed up his wooden columns, wooden panels and bits of stone, and took them with him with the rest of his furniture.

We pass from the pillared hall into the central portion of the house (34). Here we find ourselves in a lofty, regular apartment, at least 30 feet square, which obviously serves as the main drawing-room and dining-room combined. It has painted wooden pillars, four in number, taller than the pillars in the hall: which explains why, viewed from the garden, the central part of the house stands higher than the rest of it. Between the pillars, on a raised hearth, is the small brazier which holds the fire that will be needed in the wintertime; and facing the hearth, occupying almost the whole of one wall and projecting nearly as far into the room as one of the pairs of pillars, is a low raised platform. Here the owner of the house, his family and his guests will recline on rugs and cushions to talk, take their ease and eat their meals. Near at hand a second smaller platform is furnished with an array of handsomely-decorated water-jars and pots of unguent. It is the custom for people to pour a little water over their hands before they eat, or to anoint themselves before worshipping at the small concealed shrine that is probably somewhere near at hand. The shrine will be hidden in an alcove, or a room opening off the living-room, or even in the

34 The central room of a villa

living-room itself—perhaps behind the closed doors of what looks like a decorated cupboard on the far wall.

In this central living-room, as in the hypostyle halls of the temples, the windows are small and situated high up in the wall. In a country where the sunlight is as merciless as it is in Egypt there is no call for the picture-windows which are popular in countries like our own, where the light is weak. It is also no accident that the much-used living-room is situated in the middle of the house, enclosed on all sides by a mass of smaller rooms. It thus receives the benefit of retaining the heat in the winter and repelling it in summer.

In the third and rearmost portion of the house, behind the living-room, is the private suite of the master of the house and his family. If we peep into the various rooms, we will see the main bedroom; the robing-room; the bathroom with its neatly devised pipes and plumbing, its modern-looking lavatory seat, and the stone slab on which one lies to be washed and massaged;

and the office in which the master transacts the business of the estate. Well away from the family bedrooms and the office are located the well-stocked larders and the rooms allotted to the house-servants. The kitchen, with its over-pervasive odours, is sensibly situated in a separate building away from the house. Most of the servants do not live in the house itself, but in huts in the compound near the stables and workshops in which they do their work or the sheds in which they store their tools. Here too the head steward and favoured retainers will have neat little houses of their own.

We also note, in this rear portion of the house, the back door with its own ramp, and the interior ramp that leads upwards to the roof, where the family can retire to sun themselves. Some villas have attractive upper loggias or balconies that make them pleasant spots to sit and look over the wall and across the surrounding countryside. Some houses possess two or even three storeys, although the upper rooms generally possess low ceilings and are somewhat poky. And not all villas, by the way, possess ramps, but have proper staircases. The Egyptians were not, however, much given to staircases, although there was a handsome example in the South Temple at Deir el-Ballas.

35 Alabaster lamp

We might comment, as we leave the house, that it was not as lavishly decorated as we might have expected. This was an unusually spacious house, belonging to a highly-regarded member of the community, yet it possessed none of the lively frescoes which are so much in evidence in the temples and palaces. The talents of the best artists, of course, have been commandeered for the buildings of royalty, and are not usually available for the dwellings of lesser citizens. The main decoration in our villa has consisted of patterned friezes near the top of the rooms; dados of beautifully wrought faience tiles or of wood panelling; and painted ceilings in the principal hall and central living-room. In the main bedroom was a gay

72

12-foot-long mural depicting geese and ducks in flight, painted on plaster and mounted in a wooden frame on the wall behind the bed. Otherwise the walls were covered with a flat wash in a tasteful pastel shade. Here again we are reminded that the chief thoughts and energies of the individual Egyptian, particularly an Egyptian of high rank, are focused on the palaces and temples in which they perform their daily duties.

Outside, we just have time for a stroll around the garden. Tucked away in one corner is a charming little building, resembling a summerhouse, that immediately catches our eye (*36*). It has a portico with twin pillars, behind which is a door. The building is a shrine, although the devotees also like to loll in the shade of the two old tamarisk trees that flank it when, on limpid summer evenings, they come to pour over the image a leisurely libation of milk or honey.

The garden, arranged around its central pool, is mature and immaculate, the product of an age-long tradition of horticulture. There are willows, sycamores, pomegranates, figs, persea trees and two varieties of palm trees, all disposed with the eye to effect of a skilled gardener. Choice specimen trees and bushes have been planted in pots of painted earthenware. There is a row of beehives and, behind the house, a congregation of tall conical structures with square holes near the top and bottom

36 A garden shrine

which are the granaries in which the wheat and barley are stored under the watchful supervision of the overseer.

The gleaming villa, dreaming in the sun, with its range of trim whitewashed outbuildings and its lovingly tended garden, makes a perfect picture of peace and wellbeing. It is little wonder that the people who lived and laboured in such surroundings should have represented so mild and tolerant a civilisation.

TOMBS

A very significant amount of our knowledge of ancient Egypt is derived from its tombs. Indeed, it is fair to say that tombs probably loom larger in our estimate of Egypt than palaces, temples and pyramids. Can we, therefore, really claim, as we would like to do in this book, that the Egyptians were a happy people, when the tomb seems to have been the starting-point of almost all Egyptian thought and architecture? Without the tomb-chamber at its core the pyramid would have been meaningless, and the temple itself was first conceived as a mere adjunct to the pyramid-tomb.

However, it had already become apparent, from the earliest days of the New Kingdom, that the usefulness of the pyramid was exhausted. Pyramids were far too conspicuous. The pharaohs realised that the only way to try to foil their persistent enemies, the tomb robbers, was to try to hide their tombs completely. Tuthmosis I, following a hint given him by the founder of the Theban dynasty, Amenophis I, built himself a tomb with no visible superstructure whatever. His mortuary chapel was situated elsewhere: and it was this revolutionary separation of the royal tomb and the mortuary temple that quickly gave rise to the independent existence and individual evolution of the temple. We can see, therefore, that the temple, like the pyramids, also had its tap-root in the tomb.

Burial-grounds are melancholy places, even to people who believe strongly in a life beyond the grave. The Egyptians none the less devoted themselves to their burial-grounds with an extraordinary passion. Their kings, princes and officers of state often chose the site for their sepulchres when they were very young men. They spent a lifetime collecting together their grave-goods with the assiduity of a future bride tucking things away in her bottom drawer. Their notion of a pleasant little outing was to take their wives and children to see how work was progressing on the family mausoleum. It is possible that ancient Egypt was the one civilisation that has ever existed where undertakers were regarded as popular and congenial members of society.

When we turn to Egyptian religion, we must admit that the Egyptian view of life after death certainly possessed its gloomier aspects. In the prehistoric era and during the Old Kingdom ordinary people had no prospect of going to heaven at all: it was a privilege reserved exclusively for pharaoh and a few of his most favoured intimates and dependents. They alone were entitled to enter the boat of the sun-god Ra and sail away into the easternmost part of the sky to dwell among the immortals. It was only when the loosening of the exceptional authority of the kings of the Old Kingdom allowed the worship of the 'democratic' god Osiris to assert itself that the population in general secured the right of entry into the Next World. Even then the dead Egyptian had to endure fearful ordeals. The ship of death that brought him down the dark flood of the subterranean Nile, sailing beneath the cities of Egypt, had to encounter many hazards before it brought him safe home to the Celestial Fields. When he crossed the mountain range of death, and began his journey through the Underworld, he knew that he could not reach the abode of bliss unless he crossed a region haunted by fiends and monsters. If he shrank back, he would be seized, tortured and at last devoured or cremated.

And when he reached the end of the journey he had to face the sternest test of all: his trial in the Hall of Maat, goddess of Truth(37). The goddess would place his heart in one pan of her pair of scales, and in the other pan she would put the magical feather that was her sacred emblem. Then the dog-headed god Anubis would adjust the balance and the ibis-headed god Thoth would prepare to record the result on his roll of papyrus. And the jury of forty-two Assessors—one for each of the sins that could disqualify him from the delights of eternity—watched solemnly as the trial began. If the heart and feather exactly balanced one another, the issue was a triumphant success. The god Horus would step forward to conduct the lucky petitioner into the presence of Osiris, the great Prince of the West, who rested patiently within his shrine wrapped in a winding-sheet.

37 The dog-headed god Anubis, watched by the Devourer, weighs the heart of a dead man against the Feather of Truth

But if the balance tilted, if the heart was heavier than the feather, then disaster occurred. The dreadful figure of the Devourer would appear swiftly on the scene— an obscene beast with the head of a crocodile, the forepart of a lion and the hindquarters of a hippopotamus— and he would crunch the bones and munch the flesh and drink the blood of the wretched sinner.

Reaching heaven was obviously an enterprise that was fraught with anguish and peril. Is this, we ask again, the attribute of a happy people? We can only reply that the Celestial Fields were, when one had managed to scramble into them, well worth the struggle. The future prospect was glorious. After all, the priests of many ancient civilisations held out to their people no hope of heaven at all: witness the Psalmist's, 'The dead praise not Thee, O Lord, neither all they that go down into silence'. Others proffered a heaven that was barely distinguishable from hell: witness the twilit realm in which the wretched Babylonians were condemned to roam, drinking filthy water and eating muck. But the fortunate Egyptians were able to spend eternity in the Field of Rushes and the Field of Offerings, surrounded by their dear ones, free to potter about the shining meadows or cruise up and down the celestial Nile in the company of their friends. There was no doubt in their minds what heaven would be like: it would be like the kingdom of Egypt; the Two Fields were the counterpart of the Two Lands. The Egyptians had a clearer picture of their elysium than the Christians of the Middle Ages had of the Heavenly City. One might argue that to view the Next World as the counterpart of this one simply implies a lack of imagination. One might also argue that it represents a tremendous compliment to the way of life of the ancient Nile valley. The Egyptians liked it so much that they wanted it to go on for ever.

We might also note that the burial-places of ancient Egypt are among the least depressing examples of their kind. It is not at all a distasteful experience to spend days, weeks, or even months studying the sepulchres of the Egyptians. They do not engender the repulsion and horror that grip one when straying among the stained slabs and tilted crosses of Highgate or Kensal Green. The weedy and sodden cemeteries of Northern Europe breathe an atmosphere of despair—an atmosphere quite alien to the tombs of the valley of the Nile. True, the warmth, dryness and radiance of the Egyptian climate do much to strip the trappings of death of their capacity to appal. Yet one wonders whether, for example, the regimented cemeteries of the dead of World War Two that stud the western borders of the Nile will ever possess a tithe of the fascination and—yes—the appeal that characterise the cemeteries of ancient Egypt. Few people would wish to turn the leaves of a volume illustrating the tomb-stones which are crushed together in one of our typical modern cemeteries; but to pore over reproductions of the wall-paintings in the Valley of the Kings or the Valley of the Queens is a real delight (96). They are so fresh and delicate, so full of wit and vitality. Even to gaze on the dead bodies of the people who once occupied these tombs is by no means a mournful experience. Their mummy cases (40), cartonnage masks, linen wrappings, funerary furniture (39)

38 Detail from a Theban tomb painting

77

and sarcophagi are often objects of unusual beauty and artistic merit. They do not give off the stench of mortality that usually clings to the paraphernalia of the grave. The eyes that stare from the masks regard death with a gentle smile. It was not death itself that the Egyptians regarded with terror. They dreaded their fellow mortals—the impious, greedy, ignorant thieves who would come creeping into the cemeteries to ravage their remains. But in any case, they possessed the secret of contemplating death without flinching. They did not, as we are prone to do, push it away into a corner of the mind and pretend that such an unpleasant phenomenon does not exist. Some scholars believe that the Egyptians were a sceptical race, regarding the idea of death with heavy hopeless resignation, and viewing their ponderous religion with the same cynical eye as, say, the Romans. One might only indicate that much of the evidence available to us may equally well suggest that the Egyptians' view of life enabled them to confront the prospect of death with a certain buoyancy of spirit; and that, far from regarding their religion as a sham and a fantasy, it was a perpetual source of consolation to them.

From the appearance of their tombs, it would seem that the religion of the Egyptians had a certain affinity with the shintoism of Japan. Like the Japanese of the classical era, the Egyptians had a marked taste for ceremony and were devoted ancestor-worshippers. The constant, ever-present sense which the Egyptians had of the past is one of the reasons which make it hard for us to understand them. The British like to think that they are a highly conservative people, with a reverence for tradition: but even the British are a race of eager, forward-looking go-getters in comparison with the ancient Egyptians. It is very difficult for people who live in the modern world to grasp what it means to exist, as the Egyptians did, at a point in time and space where past and present intersect and are inseparable from one another. The cemetery was a place which the Egyptian was glad to visit in order to bring offerings to his forefathers whom, though dead, he still regarded as members of his family circle.

For the well-to-do Egyptian, whose tomb has survived and is visible to us today, a journey to the cemetery was no more harrowing than a journey to the private house of a neighbour or

39 The chair of Tutankhamon, Eighteenth Dynasty, showing the
Pharaoh and his wife Ankhesenamon
From Tutankhamon's tomb in the Valley of the Kings, Thebes

41 *Ushabti* of a woman holding a *Ba*-bird, Dynasty XIX

40 Mummy-case of a priestess, Dynasty XXIX

42 *Ushabti* of Tutankhamon, Dynasty XVIII

relative. The tomb was a man's 'house of eternity' in the same way that a *mastaba* or pyramid was the 'house of eternity' of his sovereign. Since it was a house that he would occupy for an immeasurably longer time than his earthly habitation, he took steps to ensure that it was decked out in an engaging manner and stocked with all the items his body would need in the tomb and his soul would need in the Elysian Fields(*44*).

If the Egyptian sometimes showed a certain disregard for earthly matters, he took the liveliest interest in all the details of life after death. For example, we ourselves usually entertain only the sketchiest notion of the nature and destination of our souls: but the Egyptians, on the other hand, distinguished between at least four different types of soul, and treated each one with considerable spiritual technicality. Thus an individual person possessed not only a *Ka*, or primary soul, but other souls as well. The *Ka* was born simultaneously with a man's body and was instantly reunited with it at his moment of death. After his death, the *Ka* lived in the tomb with the mummy, feeding on the daily offerings provided by the priests or pious relatives. Its dwelling place was the statue of the deceased person which was enclosed in the inner shrine. The second soul was the *Ba*, which emerged from the body at death to wander abroad and could select any shape it chose(*41*). If the *Ka* represented the union of the body and the life-essence, then the *Ba* was regarded as akin to the actual spiritual self. Third came the *Akh*, or 'effective spirit', whose special task was to undertake the journey to the Next World and to taste the joys of heaven. And fourth, there was the *Sekhem*, which seems to have been a twin of the *Ka*.

In the tomb, therefore, a man had to provide for his earthbound *Ka* and for his *Akh* in its sojourn in the Celestial Fields. As they were a hard-headed folk, the Egyptians stuffed their tombs with everything that they could possibly require. Among other items, they took food and drink; they took their best chairs and bedsteads; they took scores of magic spells and selected light reading; they took games and pastimes; they took

43 A *ushabti* figurine

81

their nicest clothes and choicest jewels; and they took sets of those pretty miniature figures of peasants called *ushabtis* (*41–3*). These were made of stone, wood or faience, and the word means 'answerers'. Thus when the dead man was called upon to do his individual stint in the heavenly fields, he could call up his 'answerers' to perform the task for him. A sensible arrangement.

The more important cemeteries of Egypt are too numerous to list individually. Among early examples we ought, however, to mention several outstanding groups of rock-cut sepulchres, including those of the provincial rulers of the Sixth Dynasty at distant Aswan or Elephantine, above the First Cataract; the rulers of the Hare Nome at Deir el-Bersheh; and those of the rulers of the Oryx Nome at Beni Hasan. (The nomes, of which there were nearly forty, were the counties or districts of Egypt; the word is Greek. They each had their separate symbol or totem, and retained their ancient cults and traditions. They were perhaps the remaining vestiges of the original clans or petty states that coalesced in prehistoric times to form the united realm of Egypt.)

Like the similar tombs of regional governors at Meir and Qaw el-Kebir, tombs at Beni Hasan date from the time of the Twelfth Dynasty, during the Middle Kingdom. All four groups of tombs were situated in Middle Egypt, perhaps the most stable area of the country during a politically unsettled period. The tombs at Qaw lay on the shelf of land between the Nile and the cliffs, and copied the regal style of the pyramid tombs of the late Old Kingdom. There was no pyramid, but a valley temple beside the water was connected by means of the familiar causeway to a large enclosed upper temple. The actual burial chambers were cut out of the rock behind the temple, a feature taken from the enormous pyramid-temple constructed at Deir el-Bahri by the great king Mentuhetep of the preceding dynasty. Mentuhetep's temple was daring and unorthodox in design, with the cone of the pyramid rising from long tiered terraces. At Beni Hasan, where some of the tombs go back in time to the distracted era known as the First Intermediate Period, the rock-cut tombs were magnificently sited where a bend in the river gave a superb view. The wall-paintings there afford us a piquant glimpse of every phase of Middle Kingdom life. Here the fact that the 'house of the dead' was an elaborate replica of the 'house of the living' is clearly brought home to one as one gazes at the porticos and fretted ceilings carefully cut out of the rock. Instead of the perishable columns and ceilings of wood, plaster and matting, the builders of the tombs had provided the occupants with villa-type dwellings constructed out of permanent materials.

Eventually, the rock-cut tomb became standard for the upper classes. For kings, indeed, the tomb became not simply a rock-cut house but a rock-cut palace. The small three-room sepulchre hewn for Tuthmosis I established a type that grew in size throughout the Eighteenth Dynasty. In these tombs the entrance gives on to a steeply-descending stairway, then a small ante-room, then a large pillared hall with store-rooms opening off it. In the Nineteenth Dynasty the Ramessides gradually lengthened and broadened the tomb until it reached an apogee in the tremendous and brilliantly-decorated hypogeum of Seti I. Burrowed out of the rock to a total distance of over 300 feet, its four ramps and five staircases bore downwards through four pillared halls until they culminate in the tomb chamber.

44 A room with funeral furniture inside a rock-cut tomb

When the Theban autocrats of the New Kingdom decided to construct their rock-cut tombs in the celebrated Valley of the Kings (in Arabic, Bîbân el-Molûk, or Gates of the Kings), their original aim was to secure maximum secrecy. The valley lies behind the mountain barrier on the west bank of the Nile, opposite Thebes(25). It is tucked away in a lonely fold of the cliffs, and debouches behind Deir el-Bahri into the bare wastes of the desert beyond. As Ineni, a famous architect whose labours are still prominent at Karnak, tells us in an inscription: 'I supervised the excavation of His Majesty's [i.e. Tuthmosis I's] tomb in the hills, secretly, with no one to see and hear.'

At first, extraordinary precautions were taken to conceal the entrances of the valley tombs. To no avail. The tomb robbers, who had banded together into brotherhoods and evolved techniques as ingenious as those of modern bank robbers, once again proved equal to the challenge. So the harassed pharaohs fell back on the old devices of dummy passages and dummy sarcophagi, and provided huge stone slabs in the ceiling that were meant to crash down across the passages and squash or trap the bandits. But it was all no use, even though today we often marvel at the fantastic precautions taken by the pharaohs to protect their dead bones. We ought to remember, however, that the Egyptians believed that if a man's mummy was defiled or destroyed, then the *Ka*, the *Ba*, and the other components of the soul would perish. They also believed that the survival of the Two Lands depended on keeping intact the bodies and memories of former kings, sages and great statesmen who, even when they were dead, could strengthen and bestow spiritual blessings on their former realm. Their sense of the absolute necessity of securing strict continuity from one generation to the next is an emotion that we cannot easily grasp.

Ironically enough, it was because a number of modern tomb robbers fell out with one another that a spectacular find was made at Deir el-Bahri in 1881. Two rival dynasties of tomb-robbers—and their dynasties have long outlasted the dynasties of the pharaohs—quarrelled about the disposal of a rich royal deposit; the affair finally came to the notice of the Turkish authorities, and then to the notice of a resident German Egyptologist, the great Emil Brugsch. There were denunciations, betrayals, confessions—and finally Emil Brugsch was brought to investigate an unrecorded tomb in the Bîbân el-Molûk. Here, in the square chamber of the tomb, he unearthed the remains of more than two dozen kings, queens, princes, princesses and high officials. Their bodies had been crammed higgledy-piggledy into the chamber, together with an immense quantity of furniture, chests, jars and vases. They had obviously been secretly transferred thither, late in dynastic history, in order to try to forestall the attentions of the professional criminals. The find, containing as it did the mummies of five pharaohs of the Eighteenth, three pharaohs of the Nineteenth, and Ramses III of the Twentieth Dynasty, caused a profound sensation. Is it not deeply pathetic to think of the pious officials who, so long ago and in the dead of night, assembled secretly together to deposit in one modest tomb the insulted bones of the mighty? In fact it seems to have been a frequent occurrence. We know, for example, that the mummies of some dead kings were moved in this manner at least three times. What then was the point in building a huge rock-cut tomb if one's miserable carcase was destined to be stacked in a wretched pit? Or displayed in a glass case in Boston or Bloomsbury? Or if the very lid and shell of one's coffin were wrenched apart and separated—like the coffin of Ramses III, one half of which is at Paris and the other half at Cambridge?

All the kings of the New Kingdom, with the exception of the heretic king Akhenaton, were buried in the Valley of the Kings. There were over thirty of them, and together they reigned for almost five centuries. And all their tombs were robbed, with only one single exception—the tomb of the little king Tutankhamon. And as the kings of Egypt were reckoned, the boy Tutankhamon, apart from the honour due to him as the holder of a great office, was a cipher, a nonentity, an adolescent puppet. After he died his funerary equipment was bundled into his tomb in a hasty and almost contemptuous fashion. From us today that equipment calls forth gasps of wonder: but to the ancient Egyptians it was very small beer indeed. What then must the untouched splendours of the tomb of a Snofru, or a Seti I, a Tuthmosis III or a Ramses II have been like? One's imagination is numb.

The royal tombs are situated at the far end of the Bîbân el-Molûk. Carved into the rock at the neck of the valley are a series of tombs of courtiers and politicians of the Eighteenth Dynasty that in many respects overshadow the royal tombs in interest. Here are the sepulchres of the viziers, the friends and trusted advisers of the pharaohs. The walls and ceilings of a score of them still glow with paintings or glimmer with limestone frescoes that delineate every facet of the life of Egypt in

85

the time of its fullest effulgence. To step into the halls of the great courtiers Rekhmira or Kenamon, Menena, Amenemhab, Senmut, Horemhab or Intef, is to step back across the gulf of three and a half thousand years. It is to make friendly contact with the social and intellectual aristocracy of Egypt. It is to be presented with a unique, dazzling panorama of the everyday life of a long dead people.

45–6 Inlaid faience decorations

Chapter III

THE HOME

DRESS

FROM the frescoes in the palaces and temples, and from the murals and furnishings in the tombs, we can see that the typical Egyptian tended to be slender, broad-shouldered, long in the hands and feet, and with muscular arms and legs. He was usually square-chinned and wide-lipped, with a broad forehead, large eyes, and a nose that was often somewhat short and hooked. Whether he was partly Asian by descent and lived in Lower Egypt, or partly African and lived in Upper Egypt, in both cases he appears to have been brown-haired and light-skinned. From time to time the frescoes and monuments depict the invaders who ruled Egypt at various periods, and we can discern that they possessed widely different physical characteristics: the negroid features of the pharaohs who hailed from Nubia or the Nubian border; the bedouin appearance of the Libyan kings; the semitic features of the nomadic Hyksôs or 'Shepherd Kings'. The Egyptians, like most shut-away people (e.g. the insular British of Elizabethan days), were always fascinated and diverted by foreigners, and any trader or traveller who went down into Egypt was sure to have his portrait painted in meticulous and often malicious detail. Foreigners, like dwarfs, animals and acrobats, provided the painter with a welcome change from the routine repertoire of native subjects.

The Egyptian artists also recorded the entire range of Egyptian fashions in dress, from the *haute couture* of the court to the loincloths of the peasants. Prominent as the focal point of every important mural, or the centrepiece of every group of statues, would be the figure of the king. In the plain-living and high-thinking days of the Old Kingdom, the king is depicted with his body bare to the waist: a king who is ready for work, despising effeminate frills. Even in the self-indulgent days of the New Kingdom and Late Dynastic Period, the royal limbs are wrapped in the simple robe which was the common apparel. What really

87

47 The White Crown of Upper Egypt

marks him off from the subjects who surround him is, as you will see from the paintings, the distinctive crown that he wears. If you look through a picture book of Egyptian art, you will see that in actual fact the pharaoh is endowed with a wide variety of crowns, and you may be able to count as many as 20 in all. One of those most frequently portrayed is the White Crown of Upper Egypt—a tall, graceful, conical hat of stiff white linen(47). The White Crown is also the crown invariably worn by the god Osiris, the King of the Dead, who owed his status as a national god chiefly to the hold which his cult had come to exercise over the minds of the citizens of Upper Egypt(84). In addition to the White Crown, the king also possessed a Red Crown, which was the national diadem of Lower Egypt. This was a round flat-topped cap with a tall upright projection rising from the back and ornamented in front with a curving strip of metal ribbon.

On ceremonial occasions the king wore the Red or White Crown, according to whether his dynasty hailed from Lower or Upper Egypt; and sometimes the two individual crowns were combined together into the rather ungainly Double Crown, symbolising the union of the two kingdoms. At other times the king's headdress was garnished with two stiff feathers, to signify his relationship with the falcon-god Horus, with the goddess of Truth, Maat, and also with a potent primitive chieftain called Anzti whose form and functions had been taken over by Osiris. And for very important festivals, when the king wished to place special emphasis on his kinship with Osiris or with the ram-headed god Khnum, who had fashioned the world upon a potter's wheel, he would wear an extraordinary and intricate headdress known as the *atef*-crown. Like the Crown of St Edward, the *atef*-crown must have been heavy and ill-balanced, and have more or less immobilised its wearer. It consisted of the White Crown flanked by sweeping feathers, ram's horns and

88

sacred snakes, the whole besprinkled with discs representing the sun. It is hardly surprising that in the New Kingdom this bewildering collection of royal headgear fell largely into abeyance, and gave way to the practical and attractive *khepresh* or Blue Crown(*74*). The Blue Crown, made of moulded leather studded with gold sequins, was encircled by the uraeus or sacred cobra. The cobra was the emblem of the goddess Buto, patroness of Lower Egypt, who in turn was associated with the vulture-goddess Nekhebet, patroness of Upper Egypt. Thus the cobra, with its encircling wings and disc of the sun, represented the indissoluble union of pharaoh and his two kingdoms.

Among the other regalia which are depicted by the artist, one ought to mention the false beard. Unlike their neighbours to the north-east, the Egyptians do not appear to have possessed the hairiness of Esau and his brothers; they were not remarkable for body hair and prided themselves on being clean-shaven, using well-made razors which they kept in neat leather cases(*48*). Thus the plaited beard, which could be attached to the sidepieces of royal wig or crown, was actually an artificial one. Its purpose is obscure. It may have been meant to remind pharaoh and his people of what they believed to be their racial origins in the interior of Africa, where the Nile flowed out of the land of Punt whose inhabitants were heavily bearded. But there is no mystery about those other symbols of royal power: the crook and the flail. These warned the king's subjects that, although from earliest nomadic days he had been an ever-watchful shepherd who had guided and guarded them, he could also if need be goad them forward by means of a less tender instrument.

The head-covering which we most often associate with pharaoh is, perhaps, the *nems*. This was the simple striped cloth placed round the wig, brought across the forehead and behind the ears, and tied at the base of the neck, leaving two lappets to fall forward over the shoulders on to the chest. Wigs were in fact a very prominent article of upper-class apparel. In

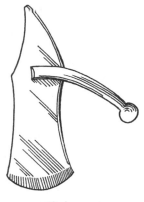

48 A razor

89

49 Men's and women's hairstyles

that hot climate, men generally wore their hair cropped short, or even shaved close, although on important occasions they would don elaborately curled, combed and pomaded wigs. In any event, they took a pride in seeing that their hair was carefully groomed and combed, in marked contrast to the hair of the unkempt and barbarous foreigner. Generally women too embellished their already complicated coiffures with wigs of ample dimensions, adorning them still further with hair-bands of beads or metal, or tasselled ribbons and tiaras(49). The wigs of both sexes are frequently seen with a white conical object perched on top of them. We are not altogether sure what this was, but it may have been a cone of solidified wax, impregnated with perfume. As the banquet or gala evening progressed, the cone would melt, and the face and neck of the wearer was laved with a delicious scent.

In a country where the majority of the inhabitants wore loin-cloths, or simply walked about naked, the basic garment of the upper classes was the robe of white linen. Men wore it over their loincloth and women over their petticoat or shift. The peasants did not even possess a robe for high days and festivals, and wore the loincloth winter as well as summer. Mostly they went naked, like their wives, sisters and daughters who worked in the great houses. The Egyptian attitude towards nudity was unselfconscious. Princes ran around naked like the children of the poor, and noblemen would wear the simple loincloth in the privacy of their houses or when pottering around their estates.

90

For ceremonial purposes, the most coveted garb was a robe of 'fine linen of Upper Egypt'. The robes of a rich man or woman would be tailored with the deceptive simplicity which a length of plain material can assume in the hands of a Paris dressmaker, and the Egyptians were experts in the arts of pleating, crimping, gauffering, and making accordion pleats. A man's robe was supported by means of shoulder-straps, or worn loose and tied at the waist with a wide strip of linen. The belt was knotted in such a way as to give the effect of a kind of triangular apron or kilt. Sometimes women would prefer, instead of a sari-like robe, a tight-fitting linen tunic resembling a modern summer frock.

50 Full ceremonial dress

Although the robe itself was artless and functional in style, it was enhanced by a colourful array of necklaces and bracelets. The Egyptians, rich or poor, men as well as women, were passionately addicted to jewellery. They were also a remarkably superstitious race, and the jewels that swayed and clinked on their necks and wrists served a magical as well as an aesthetic purpose. Pretty rings and brooches were not only nice to look at, but if they were modelled in the form of the life-giving *ankh* or the eye of Horus they could also prevent sickness and ward off the evil eye.

Egyptian jewellers were marvellously skilled. Their best work has never been surpassed, and their masterpieces bear comparison with those of a Cellini or a Fabergé. The goldsmiths of the Twelfth Dynasty, for example, achieved an extraordinary standard of excellence, and their pieces are marked by a delicacy and refinement which is sometimes lacking in the jewels that reflected the later, heavier taste of the Empire. We are fortunate

51 A princess's crown

in possessing a number of wonderful specimens of their handiwork. From the tomb of the Princess Khnumet, the daughter of Amenemhat II, who was buried beside her father's pyramid at Dahshur was recovered a pair of delicate crowns, one of them a fairy-light circlet of gold, frothing with little cornelians and inlaid with turquoise. Also from Dahshur came the jewellery, contained originally in two ivory-inlaid caskets, which had belonged to Queen Merenit and Princess Sut-Hathor, who were buried near the pyramid of Sesostris III. The caskets contained no less than five magnificent pectorals or breast-ornaments, which had been presented to these favoured ladies by the pharaohs Sesostris II, Sesostris III and Amenhemhat III, whose royal ciphers they bear. Another Egyptian princess, Sat-Hathor-Yunet, who was buried near her father's pyramid at Lahûn, was the child of the first of these kings. A pair of pectorals found in her grave bear the names of her father and of Amenemhat III; and in addition to the pectorals the grave yielded her charming little crown, ornamented with the uraeus, the two feathers, and dainty rosettes in the form of lotus-flowers (51).

Another common article of adornment which one sees in the tomb paintings is the bead collar. This was worn in the earliest times, and consisted of rows of tubular beads divided by bands

52 Gold bangle, earrings and pendant

92

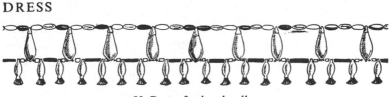

53 Part of a bead collar

of circular ones. The collar was normally at least three inches deep, but on occasion it became so broad that it covered the upper shoulders as if with a short cape. Many varied effects could be procured in the colour, arrangement, and stringing of the beads. The clasps were often elaborate, and the hawk-head of the god Horus was a popular motif for the terminals. Jewelled bracelets were worn by both sexes, and on occasion the king sported a jewelled belt adorned with his personal cartouche or cipher. Women were fond of wearing bracelets around their upper arms, as well as round the wrists and ankles. Rings, of course, were universally favoured, while earrings were fastened to the perforated lobe of the ear by means of a plug, and were sometimes so large and heavy that the whole ear was pulled out of shape. It might be mentioned, in passing, that the precious and semi-precious stones which the Egyptians employed were, in alphabetical order: agate, amethyst, beryl, calcite, cornelian, chalcedony, coral, felspar, garnet, haematite, jade, jadeite, jasper, lapis lazuli, malachite, olivine, onyx, pearl, peridot, rock-crystal, sard, sardonyx and turquoise. Diamonds, opals, rubies and sapphires were unknown.

To complete their *ensemble*, Egyptians would wear sandals of leather or woven papyrus. The sandals were usually of traditional design, with one transverse and one longitudinal thong; but occasionally the longer thong would be curved back from the toes to fasten again at the instep, like pointed shoes in

54 Necklaces

mediaeval Europe. The Egyptians were not a shoe-conscious people, and except on polite and formal occasions even noblemen would go barefoot. On the famous slate palette depicting the first pharaoh, Narmer, the king is shown barefoot, while behind him his servant carries his sandals (4). It is doubtful whether a peasant ever owned a pair of sandals in his life. However, the Egyptians had to pay for this small freedom in the penalty of many painful kinds of foot ailment, as we know from the sections that discuss these particular afflictions in the great Hearst and Ebers Papyri.

The Egyptian woman in her full glory was an awe-inspiring spectacle: the triumph of art over nature. Nature indeed had dowered her with a rare beauty: but she still found it advantageous to add innumerable little touches. In ancient Egypt the cosmetics industry was as busy as in modern Europe or America. To begin her toilet, the Egyptian lady washed her body with that thoroughness which was a fetish in Egypt. For this purpose she used a special cleansing paste, and water that was purified by the addition of salts of natron. Then, after primping and frizzing her hair to her satisfaction, she picked up her round bronze mirror with the ebony handle and started to make up her face (57). This could be a lengthy business. In the British Museum you can see the wooden toilet-case of Tutu, the wife of the scribe Ani, which is typical of many another feminine 'box of tricks' (55). Its four compartments holds jars and phials containing salves and unguents; a little palette for mixing cosmetics and eye-paint; a piece of pumice stone for removing super-fluous eyebrows or hair;

55 Wooden toilet-case of Tutu

an elbow cushion to sustain the weary arm during the course of the toilette; and an exquisite pair of pink boudoir slippers made of softest antelope leather.

When preparing to put on her 'war-paint' for the evening, Tutu would first of all pay attention to the appearance of her eyes. The 'doe-eyed' look or the almond-shaped eye was fashionable in Egypt. She would pluck out a few errant eyebrow hairs with her silver tweezers, then wet the tip of her finger or the end of a little brush and dip it in the bottle containing kohl. She would draw a thick ring round each eye, and apply more kohl to her eyelids. Until the close of the New Kingdom, kohl was manufactured from malachite, the green ore of copper; later galena, the grey ore of lead, was also widely used. When Tutu felt that her eyes were sufficiently mysterious and compelling, she would pour a little powdered red ochre on to her palette and rub it judiciously on to her

56 A noblewoman

lips and cheeks. Then she would tint her nails with henna, a dye which was in common use, as it still is today, for heightening the colour and lustre of the hair. She would also use a little henna to redden her palms and the soles of her feet. Finally she would dip a tiny spoon into an alabaster jar and anoint her skin with perfume. A large collection of subtly blended and matured perfumes was available to her. Lacking the isolates and synthetics which modern perfumiers employ as fixatives, the perfumes of Egypt were in reality scented oils. Ingredients included bitter almonds, cardamons, cinnamon, galbanum, frankincense, myrrh, sweet rush, castor oil and wine. There were many lotions for removing wrinkles and blemishes. These included preparations containing asses' milk, alabastron, natron and honey. A popular 'mud-pack' treatment was based on powdered alum.

A special word ought to be said about the peculiar beauty of

57 A bronze mirror

Egyptian toilet articles. The small personal chattels of the Egyptian man or woman were often of the most exquisite workmanship. The stone or alabaster jars and bowls which held the water for their ablutions were heirlooms, and were generally fashioned by the finest craftsmen. So were the miniature bottles, often of glass or gaily-patterned frit or faience, moulded in the entertaining shape of fishes or birds, which contained the powders and unguents. When one becomes jaded by the bulk of the pyramids and pylons, the petrified glades of the hypostyle halls, or the seemingly endless vistas of frescoes and friezes, it is always pleasant to turn to the little personal objects which the Egyptians carried about with them, or which littered their cupboards and dressing-tables. These would include their walking-sticks and riding-whips, their bows and boomerangs, their pins and combs and buttons. It is these tiny trifles, perhaps even more than the mighty monuments, that allow us to sense the true quality of their civilisation. Here there is none of that urge to impress that often induces a sensation of monotony; here the Egyptians reveal only their charm, their taste, their practicality, and their sense of humour. If one were a very wealthy man and were visited by the itch to collect, one could hardly do better than to collect, Egyptian salve-holders and perfume spoons. This small class of objects is a source of constant pleasure(59, 62). If posterity only knew about the Egyptians from their surviving monuments, there would be some excuse for believing them to

58 A perfume box

59 An elderly Nubian carrying an
unguent vase, Eighteenth Dynasty

60 A maidservant, Eleventh Dynasty
From the tomb of Meketra at Thebes

WOODEN STATUETTES

61 Bronze vessel, Dynasty XIII

62 Wooden unguent spoon, Dynasty XVIII

63 Gold jug, Dynasty XIX

64 Faience goblet, Dynasty XXII

have been stiff and pompous. But the sight of these little intimate objects immediately redeems and humanises them.

FURNITURE

The tombs of Egypt have not only revealed to us how their owners looked and acted, but have also bequeathed to us the actual movables and furniture that once graced their houses. In 1925, for example, a discovery was made near the Great Pyramid which showed that 45 centuries ago the furniture makers of Egypt were masters of their craft. In a tomb-chamber beside the pyramid causeway, the famous Egyptologist Reisner had the good fortune to unearth the funeral cache of Snofru's wife, mother of the even greater pharaoh Cheops. For some mysterious reason the body of the queen, who was called Hetephras or Hetep-heres, was not present in the narrow tomb; but Reisner recovered the elegant suite of furniture which she had used when she was alive. By careful and skilful handling he was able to restore the dry and powdery timbers to the appearance which they had originally possessed. First he disentangled and re-erected the supports and uprights of the royal canopy, which the undertakers had dismantled; then he reassembled the queen's carrying chair; finally he put together her bedstead and head-rest, her two chairs, and the other items of furniture. The bed-canopy, a present from her husband, was cased in gold. From it hung mats or curtains to provide her with privacy, and perhaps to keep out noxious insects. This was a unique find: but the pattern of the smaller pieces demonstrated that the basic design of Egyptian furniture had been formed in the Old Kingdom and were not greatly altered thereafter—another instance of the Egyptians' innate conservatism. Of course, since the shape of the human frame remains constant, the number of variations which the furniture-maker can introduce is necessarily limited; yet there are fewer points of difference between the chairs and beds found in the tomb of Hetephras and the tomb of Tutankhamon, buried more than a thousand years later, than between modern English furniture and the designs of Chippendale or Hepplewhite.

Queen Hetephras' bed sloped down towards the foot, and was provided with a head-rest(65). It is hard to believe that even the starchy dynasts of the Old Kingdom slept with a strip of

65 An ivory head-rest

wood beneath their necks, and perhaps the head-rest was used for ceremonial purposes, or to support the head of a dead person during the lying-in-state—or even during the afternoon nap in order not to disturb an elaborate coiffure. The mattress was placed on top of stretched leather thongs that served as 'springs'. The Egyptian upper classes were very proud of their beds, for to sleep in a bed was the mark of a civilised person in contrast to peasants, Asiatics or 'sand-dwellers' (i.e. Bedouins).

A similar system of leather straps was adopted for the seats of chairs, many fine examples of which have survived (66). Some of the more elaborate were four-square, with heavily decorated arms and backs, their side-panels embodying sacred figures or symbols (93). The two chairs of Queen Hetephras bear pictures of the falcon and the lotus; the chair of Tutankhamon again shows the falcon of Horus; and the chair of the princess Sitamon is adorned with the lotus, the *ankh* symbol, and a charmingly conceived ibex. The chair of Sitamon, indeed is a wholly delightful object, for it is a miniature, a child's chair, made for the little princess when she used to run about in the vast Malkata palace at Thebes. It will be noticed that the feet of these royal chairs and beds, like those of most upper-class chairs and beds, terminate in carvings of the paw of the lion: the imperial beast. Perhaps the intention was to imbue the occupiers with the animal's strength and spirit. Less important furniture usually had the legs cut straight off, like our own kitchen chairs. There were also special beds that could be taken apart, in two or three sections, and chairs with movable legs that could be neatly folded. The 'put-u-up' bed and the folding-chair are by no means recent inventions; in fact Egyptian furniture often possesses a strangely modern look. This derives not only from its general shape, but also because Egyptian *motifs* have come down to us from their influence on the plastic arts of later civilisations,

66 Everyday furniture: couch, stools, table and chairs

notably classical Rome. They also exerted a powerful influence on the architects and interior designers of eighteenth- and nineteenth-century France and England.

Although much surviving Egyptian furniture is not of the first quality, and shows that Egyptian craftsmen were not above practising 'mass-production' methods, some of it is superb. The Egyptian carpenter knew all about halved, mitred, concealed and mortice-and-tenon joints; and when he had finished his own task he passed on his handiwork to be adorned by his colleagues. The completed article was skilfully veneered, grained and painted; it was inset with decorations in metal and rare woods and inscriptions and vignettes of faience and enamel. A wonderful example of the latter is the triple inscription, inlaid in hieroglyphs of gleaming gold, which makes the back of Queen Hetephras' carrying-chair a thing of extraordinary beauty.

An ordinary upper-class household, of course, was not always enhanced with such 'status symbols' as chairs and beds. No doubt many a worthy burgher reclined on a reed mat to take his meals, and laid himself down at nights on a mattress on the floor. We must not imagine that the well-to-do Egyptian villa was overloaded with furniture, even in the 'Victorian' days of the Eighteenth Dynasty. As for the peasants, they possessed no furniture at all, and probably the majority of Egyptian dwellings seldom contained anything more remarkable than a simple pot-stand in the living-room. Wealthy indeed was a family that owned two sets of dishes, one of earthenware for everyday use, the other of schist or alabaster for 'best'. Nor were chairs or tables so common in larger houses that the host and his guests would not customarily sit together on the floor, eating the food with their fingers. There were no dining-tables in ancient Egypt, such as we use them in our own houses, and the dishes were placed on small side-tables. Even offices were seldom furnished with stools and desks, for the scribe's roll of papyrus was stiff enough for him to prop upon his knees as he squatted on the ground. Of basins and bowls for the kitchen, on the other hand, there was everywhere a plentiful supply; and it was a very poor family indeed that could not boast a set of well-carved drinking-cups and a handsome jug(64). In the later dynasties jugs and vases of gold and silver came into fashion, and were often fitted with ingenious internal strainers like modern teapots.

67 Earthenware pots and drinking vessels

Probably every household possessed at least one chest in which to keep the linen and the family treasures, and receptacles of excellent basket-ware were readily available. Many chests of splendid workmanship can be seen in modern museums, ranging from the wonderfully-executed coffers and caskets (and coffins) of the queens and pharaohs to the plain boxes of the less exalted citizens, which doubtless also did duty as divans and seats. In many houses, clothes and other belongings were often stowed away in 'built-in cupboards' of brick in the main bedrooms.

FOOD AND DRINK

When we paid our visit to the Egyptian villa, we touched briefly upon the horticultural aspects of the elegant garden in which it was set. Let us now see what that same garden would have yielded its proud owner in the more mundane matter of food and drink. The ancient Egyptians were notable trenchermen, and

68 Fig-picking

where the good things of the table were concerned, no less than with their other creature comforts, their standard of living was probably higher than it is now.

The ornamental trees around the villa bore several excellent varieties of figs and dates (*68*); and from the beginning of the New Kingdom apples and pomegranates were also cultivated. Coconuts were a luxury, while the more luscious fruits such as oranges and lemons, pears and peaches, cherries and bananas, were not grown at all during pharaonic times. If the original list of fruits seems rather exiguous, it was generously supplemented by the universal presence of the grape. In every garden a profusion of vines would be curled up poles, twined round pergolas, or trained against the wall of the house or compound. The successful tending of *vitis vinifera* requires much skill and patience, from which we can infer that the Egyptians must have possessed these qualities abundantly.

The selection of vegetables was much wider than that of fruits. There was a plentiful supply of onions, leeks, beans, garlic, lentils, chick peas, radishes, spinach, turnips, carrots and lettuces. The most suitable of these were sun-dried and stored for the winter. Cucumbers and several sorts of melons, pumpkins and gourds were also grown in large quantities. Many of these vegetables, particularly the fleshy and ever-popular lettuce, were probably served with oil, vinegar and salt, and there is no doubt that the art of dressing a salad is an ancient one. Edible oils were derived principally from the *bak* tree, at least until the late advent of the olive, while castor oil was extracted for medicinal purposes and for lighting lamps.

Meat was consumed in vast quantities. The staple meat was beef, and herds of oxen, derived from the long-horned wild ox, were specially fattened for slaughter. As in our own day, the fillet was regarded as the choicest cut. Smaller quantities of lamb and goat, the former derived from the reddish-coated Mouflon, were also eaten; and there was a limited demand for the more exotic meats that occasionally reached the larder as a result of the exertions of the huntsmen. These included the oryx, the gazelle and the ibex. Next to beef, by far the most common meats were those of birds. The wild-fowling industry was large and highly organised, particularly in the marshes of the Delta(96). Ducks, wild geese, pigeons, quails and cranes were trapped in enormous numbers, and flocks of domestic geese and ducks were hand-reared for the table(69). The taste for fish was more equivocal. Either fresh-run, or dried and salted, they were eaten in shoals by the poorer classes, for whom it was in the nature of a steady diet; and there were permanent fishing fleets at work in the Delta and the Fayûm. But in primitive communities fish are often the subject of complicated tabus, and even in dynastic times certain kinds of fish seem to have been prohibited in some of the nomes or provinces. The fact that the fish was sacred to the malignant god Seth may have induced people to treat it with caution. That tabus of this kind operated

69 Forced feeding on a poultry farm

105

70 Grape-treading, with characteristic wine jars

is indicated by the fact that the flesh of the pig was eschewed as totally unclean.

In the matter of drink the ancient Egyptian had a wide choice. We have already mentioned the cultivation of the grape, from which many varieties of wine were made (70). The Egyptians certainly liked their wines sweet, and on occasion spiced it with honey and the juice of dates or pomegranates. Wine jars with individual clay sealings occur as early as the First Dynasty. In Old Kingdom times the wines were predominantly red, but from the Middle Kingdom onwards white wine became increasingly popular. Certain vineyards acquired an enviable reputation, the wine of Buto in the Delta being particularly coveted. The inscriptions on one series of jars reads 'excellent wine of the king's growth'. Cellars of wine were systematically laid down, with the vintages carefully recorded, and the tall, tapering amphorae were racked and re-racked to improve the quality. To provide variety for their practised palates, the Egyptians also imported wine from Syria and Palestine, and later from Greece.

It is probable, of course, that wine-drinking was mainly confined to the upper classes, for the chief national drink was beer. This was manufactured by lightly baking thick loaves of wheat and barley, then allowing them to ferment in vats of water. Milk was highly prized, and so were its derivatives, butter and cheese. Eggs, on the other hand, were plentiful in view of the hundreds of thousands of birds which were caught or bred (although our own domestic hen was not known).

Wheat and barley provided the baker with the raw materials for the countless varieties of bread and cake in which he specialised. The wheat was not the widely distributed bread wheat (*triticum vulgare*) but the more restricted variety known as.

71 A rich man and his wife at dinner

emmer (*triticum dicoccum*); and the Egyptian baker worked wonders with it. With a loaf of fragrantly-smelling bread, fresh from the mould, a jug of beer and an onion, the Egyptian peasant in his reed hut could munch away with as much contentment as the nobleman enjoying an elaborate repast in his pillared hall.

Like the peasant reclining on his mat of rushes, the nobleman seated on his carved chair ate his food with his fingers. On chairs nearby sat his principal male guests, while the less important diners, the women and lesser members of the family, occupied cushions on the floor(*71*). Even pharaoh, with the little tables in front of him laden with beautifully wrought jars and vessels, would gnaw at a beef-bone while his queen picked daintily on the wing of a plover. Between courses the servants brought forward basin and ewer for the diners to rinse their hands. By our own standards, to eat with one's fingers seems uncouth and unsophisticated; but one ought perhaps to remind oneself that knives, forks and napkin-rings may not, after all, be a very profound index of a civilised condition.

TRANSPORT

This chapter would not be complete without some account of how the Egyptians travelled between their villas and town houses, their temples and palaces, their cities and cemeteries. The answer is simple: for the most part they used the river Nile(*1*).

The river was the arterial highway which rendered every province of the two kingdoms immediately accessible. Together with its network of canals, it permitted free traffic to citizens of both kingdoms and enabled men from Upper and Lower Egypt to mingle easily and continuously with each other, except at times of political upheaval. The river was thus a factor which made for uniformity and a sense of national identity.

The busy life of a great river always takes on a character of its own. The Nile was no exception. Early in Egypt's history the men of the river constituted a caste of their own. There are fine limestone reliefs from noblemen's tombs at Sakkara, dating from about 2650 B.C., which show crews building their boats, carrying their equipment home after a voyage, and fighting among themselves. The same reliefs show different types of boat, although the general shape of the hull and arrangement of the

72 The nobleman Ti hunting hippopotami from a papyrus boat

rigging of Egyptian ships were more or less fixed at the end of the predynastic period. For large vessels the hull was of timber, with carvel-built or flush planking; and for smaller and more utilitarian boats, such as rafts and punts, bundles of papyrus reeds were lashed together with ropes. The nobleman Ti, one of the Sakkara noblemen to whom we have referred, is shown hunting the hippopotamus in one of these papyrus boats (72).

Egyptian craft had a low, curved prow and a high stern. The ends of both prow and stern were often curled into the form of a papyrus flower, a decoration invariably employed on the ornate, steep-sided, painted and gilded funeral barges, like huge Venetian gondolas, which ferried the mummies of wealthy citizens to the sacred necropolis of Abydos or some other holy burial-ground (12). The mast was placed centrally and the wide lateen sail, almost as long as the ship, was operated by a specially-trained sailor seated on the awning or on the poop at the stern, twitching a lanyard to keep the sail filled with the breeze. Also at the stern, on a special platform, stood the steersmen, who might number as many as four in the case of larger vessels, plying their long narrow paddles; and on the prow stood the pilot or look-out, watching for shoals, and either taking soundings himself with his pole or accompanied by a sailor deputed to do so. In the centre of the ship, or somewhere near the bow, there was usually an awning of some kind, either of wood or canvas or rushes; for on those shadowless waters a patch of shelter was in the nature of a necessity. Amidships were the rowers, standing or kneeling in two rows on the deck facing the stern, and equipped with curved broad-bladed oars. They rowed in time to a flute, a gong, a rattle, or a hoarsely-reiterated shanty. The size of the crew varied. The enormous argosies in which pharaoh made his royal progress required 40 or 50 men, while the little ships which plied merrily backwards and forwards as common carriers required only two or three. These small but sturdy craft might be carrying a consignment of wine or corn, with an oxen or two thrown in for good measure. In addition to boats, the river was thronged with enormous rafts. Many of them had been constructed for special purposes, such as to float down the Nile the stone needed for erecting pyramids,

73 A large boat under sail, with the rowers resting on their oars

colossal statues and obelisks. One of these rafts was capable of bearing over 600 tons of stone, and there is record of another which was 100 feet long, 50 feet wide, and was built in seventeen days. The Egyptians were used to building large vessels. In the Fourth Dynasty, one of King Snofru's ships was 100 cubits, i.e., 172 feet, in overall length.

What of transport on land? In that watery country, where canals took the place of major and minor roads, land conveyances were not so important. A commonly seen vehicle was the carrying-chair or palanquin, of the type of which Queen Hetephras of the Old Kingdom owned such a beautiful example. For travelling long distances the sides of the palanquin were boarded or covered with linen panels, like the *daks* in which officials journeyed through British India less than a century ago; but for shorter trips the palanquin was simply a chair placed on a platform carried high on the shoulders of pole-bearers, the sedan chairmen of their age. In this fashion we often see pharaoh borne aloft through the throng on his state throne in exactly the same manner as the modern Popes are borne through the multitudes within the precincts of St Peter's.

Chariots, as we shall see in the next chapter, were a relatively late innovation, and were used purely for military purposes or for hunting(*91*). The ancient Egyptians were not horsemen but sailors. Here again, however, their natural conservatism asserted itself, for although they loved the freshwater flood of their native river, they had less stomach for the broad sheet of water that nibbled the shores of the Delta. The sea-going abilities of Egyptian sailors are sometimes under-rated; they seem to have ventured out into the Atlantic, beyond the Pillars of Hercules, and even to have made a circumnavigation of the African continent. But it seems fair to say that in general they regarded the tidal and treacherous expanse of the Mediterranean with deep-seated antipathy. They called it 'the Great Gren'; and if they were forced to make the voyage to Tyre, they took care to hug the coastline the whole way along. They believed for the most part that, if the barbarians wanted to purchase or barter their wares for the wares of the Black Land, then let them risk their own necks and come and fetch them.

111

Chapter IV

PEOPLE AND PROFESSIONS

THE government of Egypt was feudal and theocratic. Every thread and filament of social and spiritual authority ran back directly to the hand of the king. The slightest twitch which he gave to the reins of authority was felt from end to end of his kingdom. He was the cone that topped the structure of the Egyptian pyramid. In lands like Babylonia the king was a mere mortal who was chosen by the gods to act as their representative on earth. The king of Egypt was a god in his own right. To be more accurate, he was many gods. He was not only the incarnation of his father, the protean sun-god Ra; he was also identified with Ra's son, the falcon-god Horus(81). And Horus in turn had a curious dual personality. As the local deity of Hierakonpolis, he was the totem of an Upper Egyptian nome which at the opening of the dynastic epoch is believed by some historians to have conquered Lower Egypt and brought about the union of Egypt. Later the priests of Heliopolis merged the worship of this historical Horus with a legendary Horus who was the son of Osiris, Lord of the Dead. So when pharaoh died he was held to be resurrected as Osiris (or, rather, as *an* Osiris). Thus he was not only Ra and Ra's son Horus, but also Osiris and Osiris's son Horus, all at one and the same time. A confusing situation, admittedly: but one which indicates the rich aura of sanctity with which successive generations of theologians had invested the ruler of Egypt. No person was ever so hedged about as pharaoh with the divinity that doth hedge a king.

Every morning at dawn pharaoh would go into the House of the Morning, one of his private chapels. There he would perform a ritual laving of his limbs. In the way that the sun-god Ra bathed each morning in the primordial ocean of heaven, so pharaoh bathed his body in order to restore the vital force that flowed therefrom upon the Two Lands. Then he was anointed, robed, and invested with the royal insignia by priests wearing

113

the masks of Horus and the ibis-headed god of wisdom, Thoth. Next he proceeded to the temple, where he officiated at a further ceremony. Its aims were to implant spirituality into the ceremonies that would soon be celebrated in all the other temples throughout the land—a kind of act of transubstantiation. Pharaoh was Egypt's divine catalyst. He was a celestial sparking-plug. The Egyptians did not believe that the whole machine of living could start again at sunrise unless their god-king recited the magic words.

74 Ramses II on his throne, wearing the Blue Crown

The court of pharaoh was as solemn and hierarchical as the courts of the stiffest Bourbon or Habsburg. Pharaoh's *levées* and *couchers* were as ceremonious as those of Louis XIV. (Did not *Le Roi Soleil* unconsciously emulate Ra Harakhte?) The king's every move and gesture was endowed with drama. It was a fearful misfortune to find that his shadow had fallen upon one; and to be touched accidentally by his staff might bring very bad luck indeed, unless he was gracious enough to apologise. To be allowed to kiss his actual foot, instead of the dust in front of it, was an extraordinary mark of favour. His personal name was so sacred and fraught with magic that it was dangerous to utter it, and that was why he was called by the impersonal title of 'Pharaoh'. The word comes from the two words *per aa*, 'Great

114

House': that is, 'The Palace'. In a lesser way we still use 'Buckingham Palace' as a circumlocution for the Queen of England, and 'the White House' for the President of the U.S.A.

As a boy, his daily life was comparatively carefree. He could not foresee the cruel prison of protocol in which he would one day be shut up. He played with his companions, and was taught to swim, to ride, and to shoot with his miniature bow and arrow. As soon as he was old enough, he entered the army to serve a military apprenticeship, in company with the sons of noblemen and foreign princes who had been sent to Egypt to be educated. When the time eventually came for him to mount the throne, he would be changed from a pampered and lively princeling into a withdrawn and frightening god. Here is a description of the solemn moment when King Seti I decided to adopt the Crown Prince, who was about 15-years-old at the time, as his co-ruler.

> The Universal Lord himself [i.e. King Seti] magnified me whilst I was a child until I became ruler. He gave me the land while I was in the egg, the great ones smelling the earth before my face. Then I was inducted as eldest son to be Hereditary Prince upon the throne of Geb [the earth-god] and I reported the state of the Two Lands as captain of the infantry and the chariotry. Then when my father appeared in glory before the people, I being a babe in his lap, he said concerning me: 'Crown him as king that I may see his beauty whilst I am alive.' And he called to the chamberlains to fasten the crowns upon my forehead. 'Give him the Great One [the uraeus-serpent] upon his head', said he concerning me.

The Crown Prince ultimately succeeded his father as the pharaoh Ramses II, and reigned with awe-inspiring pomp and power for 67 years(74).

A prince or king married young, usually in childhood. He carried in his veins the actual blood of the sun-god Ra, and it was important that this divine liquid should not be diluted; so he preserved its purity and potency by marrying a member of his own family—sister, half-sister or cousin. In this he was following the example of Osiris, who had married his sister Isis. Pharaohs even occasionally married their own daughters and had children by them. On the other hand, it must not be thought that incest was a widespread practice; as in the parallel case of the royal family of the Incas, it was strictly confined to the royal circle and carried out with religious sanction. It should also be remembered that by the operation of the ancient clan system of pre-dynastic times property and possessions were transferred in Egypt through the female line, that is by matrilineal rather than patrilineal descent. Thus it was nominally the Queen or Crown Princess rather than the Crown Prince who would inherit the throne, and to secure his title to it beyond the faintest shadow of a doubt the pharaoh lost no time in marrying every woman who could possibly lay claim to the throne. He was therefore usually polygamous as well as incestuous; and in addition to his principal and much-venerated spouse, who went by the name of Great Chief Wife, he possessed a number of daughter-wives and

75 Musicians and dancers: members of the royal *harim*

sister-wives. He might also possess a further bevy of what might be called political wives: foreign princesses who had been sent by their fathers to marry the king of Egypt in order to cement a diplomatic alliance. A third group of wives would consist of the dancing girls or other ladies who had caught his fancy and had been bought and introduced into the royal *harîm*(75). These he might or might not choose to marry, and might or might not recognize their offspring as princes or princesses.

Sometimes a pharaoh might happen to be eccentric, or weak minded, or half-mad, or a child in his early teens. Sometimes the clique who actually ran the country privately despised or hated him. Yet outwardly they always took care to pay him the most scrupulous respect. They knew that the institutions of Egypt would immediately disintegrate if the character of the monarchy were damaged. For the Egyptian state to function the authority of its king must remain unimpaired. Pharaoh was the keystone of the entire edifice. As such he was endowed with exceptional power. His word was literally law; he was a Pope whose pronouncements were always *ex cathedra*. Justice was considered quite simply to be 'what Pharaoh loves', and wrong-doing 'what Pharaoh hates'. His statements were divine statutes. He was Archbishop and Lord Chief Justice combined in a single person.

Egypt was commonly fortunate in her pharaohs. She produced some remarkably able, patient and far-sighted rulers. If the kings of Egypt were gods, they were hard-working gods. The sheer weight of the burden that rested on their shoulders, the sheer scale of the challenge, evoked a corresponding response. They usually chose to take up their abode for half the year in Lower Egypt and half the year in Upper Egypt, and from their palaces at Memphis and Thebes expeditions and tours of inspection were made constantly. Their writ ran throughout the whole land by means of a separate royal bureaucracy, operating in the provincial centres side by side with the local civil servants. The conduct of diplomacy became increasingly demanding as the other nations of Hither Asia grew mightier and more threatening as the centuries rolled on. Daily, almost hourly, pharaoh would be closeted with his own senior advisers or with foreign ambassadors. Human nature being what it is, a number of pharaohs were by nature frivolous and self-indulgent, as their images and inscriptions testify; but the scribes and artists of Egypt also reveal, in spite of the habits of conventionalising and idealising, that many of the king-gods were sagacious and energetic men. Some of them seem almost bowed down to the ground by the well-nigh intolerable weight of the sacred trust which had been placed upon them. It was no sinecure to be born to rule the kingdom which had once been ruled by the gods themselves. There exist many portrait-heads of the pharaoh Sesostris III of the exceptionally gifted Twelfth Dynasty, and many of his equally illustrious successor, Amenemhat III(76). Together these two kings ruled Egypt for nearly 80 years, between 1878 and 1797 B.C. They were called upon to reign after an epoch of appalling chaos. They righted the weaknesses of the state and guided it far along the path to prosperity. The cost of that extreme personal effort has been graven by the sculptors into their stony features for us to see. The force and feeling for truth of these portrait heads place them among the *chefs d'œuvre* of the sculptor's art. When we contemplate those proud and toil-worn faces, we sense the full authority of the pharaohs of Egypt. We understand why one of Amenemhat's officers of state should have described him to his family in these terms:

> He is the god Ra whose beams enable us to see. He gives more light to the Two Lands than the sun's disc. He makes the earth more green than the Nile in flood. He has filled the Two Lands with strength and life. He is the Ka [i.e. his kingdom's guardian spirit]. He is the god Khnum who fashions all flesh. He is the goddess Bast who defends Egypt. Whoever worships him is under his protection; but he is Sekhmet, the terrible lion-goddess, to those who disobey him. Take care not to defy him. A friend of Pharaoh attains the rank of Honoured One, but there is no tomb for the rebel. His body is thrown into the river. Therefore listen to what I tell you and you will enjoy health and prosperity.

The death of a king of Egypt was always regarded as a shattering and indeed earth-shaking event. Here is the announcement of the death of Amenemhat I, the founder of the Twelfth Dynasty and inspired leader of his country for three decades, until he fell victim to a cowardly assassin.

> Year 30, third month of the Inundation season, day 7. The god mounted to his horizon. The King of Upper and Lower Egypt went

76 Amenemhat III, Twelfth Dynasty
Detail of a limestone statue from a funerary temple at Hawara

78 The sage Imhotep, vizier of King Zoser
Wooden statuette of the Third Dynasty

77 The priest and royal scribe Hesira,
Third Dynasty. *From a wooden panel in
his 'mastaba' at Sakkara*

aloft to heaven and became united with the sun's disc. The limb of the god was merged in him who made him. The Residence was hushed; hearts were in mourning; the Great Gates were closed; the courtiers crouched with their heads on their knees; and the nobles grieved.

Eloquent and sorrowful words.

NOBLEMEN AND ADMINISTRATORS

The population of Egypt possibly numbered between four and five million souls. This was a huge population for an ancient civilisation, and pharaoh had full need of his well-organized army, his police force, and his extensive civil service. His palace was not only his home, but the headquarters of the Six Great Houses, the six grand divisions of the administration. Again one is struck by the parallel with that outstanding Pharaoh of modern European history, Louis XIV. As at Versailles, if you had been a foreign ambassador, and if you had called at the palace to pay your respects to its revered occupant, you would have found a host of officials scurrying ceaselessly backwards and forwards through its courtyards and corridors. The Egyptians were devoted bureaucrats, and Egypt was one of the most efficiently ordered states that the world has ever seen.

In the early days, from the opening of the First Dynasty until the end of the Fourth (c. 3100–2480 B.C.), the kings of Egypt were able to maintain a more or less personal rule. But they governed a kingdom with a diverse and growing population, a kingdom that was over 500 miles long, most of which could only be visited by means of a long slow row against the stream. It was inevitable that sooner or later some devolution of the royal authority would have to take place. When King Zoser of the Third Dynasty decided to move the capital to Memphis, in Lower Egypt, it was only natural that the distant nobles of Upper Egypt should come to assume increasing responsibility for their own affairs. A gradually widening separation of powers between the administration of Lower and Upper Egypt seems to have occurred during the closing centuries of the Old Kingdom; and the subsequent determination of later pharaohs to reassert their authority over their own civil servants and over a cadre of barons who had grown too independent may have helped to foster the collapse and chaos of the First Intermediate Period. If we knew more about the pretensions of the provincial aristocracy, we would know more than we do about the internal stresses that sometimes afflicted the structure of the Egyptian state. Similarly, we would like to be better informed about the ramifications of the Egyptian civil service and its rivalry with the crown and priesthood. In any highly centralised state the influence of leading officials is always paramount; but senior civil servants, in all countries and in all ages, have been adept in concealing their ambitions and machinations from prying eyes. The great ones of ancient Egypt were no exception: and they have successfully kept their own counsel.

No whisper of interdepartmental frictions or jealousies reaches us from the inscriptions in the tombs. There, every blessing and benefit which the owner received during the whole course of his life is attributed directly to pharaoh. This is the officially propagated myth. In theory, these inscriptions, with their long lists of honours and titles, should give us an accurate picture of the way in which the upper echelons of Egyptian society were graded. There are titles in plenty: Klaus Baer has counted almost two thousand distinct varieties of them in the tombs of the Fifth and Sixth Dynasties alone (*Rank and Title in the Old Kingdom*).

Thus the important grandee Harkhuf describes himself in his tomb at Aswan as 'Prince, seal-bearer of the King of Lower Egypt, unique friend, lector-priest, god's seal-bearer, and confidant of royal commands'. The Egyptians were fond of adorning themselves with such impressive strings of titles; but although their general sense is often clear, it is usually difficult to associate most of them with specific roles and duties. Some of them indicate definite official functions, whereas others are purely decorative and honorific. Thus if you had been introduced to the 'Overseer of the Double Bathroom', it seems probable that you would have been meeting the equivalent of a holder of a British C.B.: and a Commander of the Bath has nothing to do with commanding bathrooms. Of course, the 'Overseer of the Double Bathroom' may have possessed some unique privilege, like holding the towel when the king stepped out of his bath— rather like those courtiers of Louis XIV who were so proud of their special right to hold the king's shirt or drawers when he got dressed in the morning. Similarly, if you had met pharaoh's 'Sandal-bearer' you would probably have discovered that he was no more than the equivalent of a member of the Most Noble Order of the Garter. On the other hand, pharaoh did possess a house-order that resembled that of the Knights of Windsor. When Harkhuf refers to himself as 'unique friend', he means that he was actually numbered among the inner group of courtiers on whom pharaoh had bestowed the title of Unique Friend or Sole Companion.

Next to pharaoh, the most important functionary was the vizier. Even the title of this exalted personage was, however, somewhat equivocal, as it appears that it was worn by various favoured princelings who could never have actually exercised the office. None the less, the names of many outstanding viziers, whose power was certainly supreme, have come down to us. Among them were Mentuhotep and Sehetepibra, who helped the great pharaohs of the Twelfth Dynasty to achieve the onerous feats which we mentioned above. Several viziers acquired such a reputation for wisdom, piety and dedication that they were worshipped in later years as gods. This select group included the sages Kagemni and Ptahhotep, who left behind them collections of wise sayings; Imhotep, the Egyptian Leonardo da Vinci, the polymath who shed lustre on the reign of King Zoser(78); and Amenhotep, philosopher and friend of Amenophis III, whose master ordered a special temple to be built to perpetuate his memory. Thus the viziers, one of whose subordinate titles shows that they were specially directed to be the 'Superintendent of all the works of the King', were sometimes accorded royal and god-like status.

Let us, during the course of a brief visit to the Great House, put our head round the door of the lofty apartment in which the vizier Rekhmira, one of the most famous law-givers of the Eighteenth Dynasty, is holding his morning *diwan*(79). There is an empty bench near the back of the room, and without attracting attention we tiptoe forward and take a seat. The court has already been in session for several hours; indeed, Rekhmira is a notoriously early riser, and likes to stroll at dawn through the sleepy streets of Thebes, communing with himself and brooding over current problems as he makes his way to his office. He has

123

79 A vizier holding his *diwan*

completed half a day's work by the time we were eating our early morning repast of dates and sweet cake. There he sits, enthroned above his bevy of executives, his flock of scribes, his Director of the Cabinet, his Keeper-of-the-things-which-come-in. The petitioners and prisoners whose cases are being heard are ranged in orderly rows at the foot of his dais, beneath the watchful eye of a pair of brawny policemen. Cases are taken in strict rotation, for one of the vizier's strictest rules is that 'Audience is not given to the man at the back before the man in front'. Many of the cases are in the nature of an appeal or a re-trial, cases that pose legal conundrums, or that have baffled the magistrates of the three lower courts, the Kenbet, the Great Kenbet or Saru, and the Zazat. Rekhmira listens with quiet concentration to the arguments which are addressed to him; now and again he ruffles back the sleeve of his linen robe with a slow gesture of his arm, as he rests his chin in his hand. The harsh morning light that floods down into the white-walled chamber from the windows high up in the wall illumines the lined and austere planes of his face. Now and again he interrupts in a low voice to request that the pleading be kept short and to

124

the point. He reminds his hearers that he has a great many cases to dispose of before noon, when he must join the Chancellor to submit his daily report to pharaoh. We notice that his manner, even to a humble peasant who comes to bewail the theft of a donkey, is calm and courteous. His verdicts are concise and couched in language which everyone can understand. He has long ago taken to heart the words of the traditional charge which the king made to him when he was inducted into his great office:

> To be vizier requires not mildness but firmness. You must not take sides with the Saru or Zazat or make any man a slave. When a petitioner comes from Upper or Lower Egypt, you must look thoroughly into his case and act in such a way that he has his rights. Remember also that an official must live with his face uncovered [i.e. his life must be an open book]. The wind and water report all that he does. Look on your friend as a stranger and a stranger as your friend. An official who acts in this way will hold his post a long time. Do not send away any petitioner unheard and do not brusquely reject what he says. If you refuse him, let him know why you refuse him. A man with a grievance likes his tale of woe to be heard sympathetically even more than he wants it put right. Do not fly into a rage with a man wrongfully. Fly into a rage only when rage is necessary. A real magistrate is always feared. If he is feared it makes court procedure more impressive. But if people are positively frightened out of their wits by him, it can do his reputation a good deal of harm. People won't say of him: 'There's a fine fellow!' You will be respected in your profession if you act strictly according to the dictates of justice.

Rekhmira's duties for the day will not be over when his *diwan* is closed, or even when he has finished his audience with pharaoh. After snatching a brief siesta, he is then due to confer with the Viceroy of Nubia, a somewhat touchy and pompous person who must be handled tactfully; and afterwards there are consultations with the governors of two important nomes who are at present on leave in the capital. Before he can return to his villa for an evening's relaxation with his family, he must also put in a solid stint in his office, attending to the accumulation of paper-work. He must scrutinise the tax returns; the receipts of the royal storehouses; the latest census of livestock and animal-feeding stuffs; and the routine reports on recent rainfall and the height of the Nile. Then there is his correspondence. Above all he must remember to write to the local superintendent of water-works about the disgraceful condition of the Theban reservoirs; to the nomarch of Asyut to confirm that his request to under-take extensive tree-felling has been refused; and to his sub-ordinate vizier in Lower Egypt to tell him to prod his provincial governors into submitting their next set of tri-annual accounts by the official date. He will have to apologise to his confidential scribes for making them work so late for the fifth or sixth night in succession. But perhaps this infernal pressure will ease a little soon? It would be pleasant to take a holiday; to see more of his wife; to do a spot of fishing with his three boys; to carry out those experiments in fruit-grafting and cattle-breeding he would have liked to have begun last summer; and to commit to papyrus some of those pithy reflections on matters of taste and conduct which have been forming in his mind during his morning walks.

Rekhmira entertains great expectations for his eldest son. The boy is shrewd and sensible, and Rekhmira hopes that one day the boy will succeed to his own exalted office. The Egyptians valued the hereditary principle in public administration no less than in kingcraft, and there were family dynasties of viziers and senior civil servants in the same way that there were dynasties of pharaohs. There were also dynasties of nomarchs, the provincial rulers of either aristocratic or bureaucratic origin who liked to abrogate to themselves semi-royal status. They were little pharaohs in their own right, and their provinces often came to resemble little kingdoms. If you had spent an hour in the courtroom of the vizier in any one of the provincial capitals, you would have recognized it as a miniature version of Rekh-mira's court at Thebes; and the vizier would have gone to make his daily report to his master in the same way as Rekhmira.

We have said that it was the pretensions of the provincial nobility which led to the breaking-up of the Old Kingdom; and it is at this time, during the Sixth Dynasty, that the nomarchs began to build themselves splendid tombs and adorn them with inscriptions betraying a hitherto unheard-of absence of servility in their attitude to pharaoh. 'I claimed from King Pepi II', states the nomarch of the Twelfth Nome at Hierakonpolis, 'the honour of obtaining a sarcophagus, funerary wrappings and oils for my father. I asked the king to make my father a prince and the king made him a prince and awarded him the Gift-which-the-King-gives.' Obviously Pepi II was eager to please such nomarchs as this, who had succeeded in making their offices hereditary instead of royal appointments. The evident weakening of royal authority and the waxing strength of the nomarchs eventually led to the internal struggles of the First Intermediate Period. This Period, a kind of Egyptian Wars of the Roses, saw the Upper Egyptian nomes, banded round the fire-eating Nomarch of Thebes, locked in battle with a confederation from Lower Egypt centred upon the Nomarch of Herakleopolis. Eventually it was the Thebans who won; and rather like the Tudors after the victory at Bosworth, the Thebans took good care to sit firmly on friend and foe alike. The Theban pharaohs of the Middle Kingdom integrated the nomes into a central system of government and managed to reduce the provincial nobility to the level of country squires, while contriving to pack the ranks of provincial governments with their own nominees. If ever a country stood in need of well-regulated central government, at that moment that country was Egypt. In times when the provincial aristocrats were too antagonistic to co-operate with one another, the whole country suffered. There was a simple reason for this. Egypt was entirely dependent on a properly organized supply of water, and the most important single task of local and central government was to ensure that the intricate system of dykes and canals was kept in constant good order. It only needed a petty squabble between a handful of petty princelings in Upper Egypt to damage the irrigation network; and the consequences would be felt far downstream in Middle and Lower Egypt. Team work and a sense of public spirit were essential.

In periods when pharaoh's power was strong, the standard of civic rule in Egypt was uniformly high; and the power of pharaoh depended in turn upon the efficiency of his administrators. The extraordinarily long periods of stability and prosperity which Egypt enjoyed are proof that efficient administrators, whether local aristocrats or career civil servants, were never in short supply. They were entitled to take a pride in the achievements of moulding an image of their country which has impressed posterity so deeply. Thus Ameni, lord of the Sixteenth

Nome of Upper Egypt, boasts in his tomb at Beni Hasan that he had

> spent years as ruler in the Oryx Nome, and performed all services on behalf of the Great House. I appointed the overseers on every estate throughout the province and charged them with the upkeep of three thousand head of cattle. When census-time came round, my efforts in this regard were duly praised by the Great House. No shortage was ever recorded against my concerning my delivery of royal quotas.

Ameni is proud to relate that his subjects had enjoyed perfect justice, that the poor woman and the widow had lived in complete security, and that he had abolished poverty and looked after agriculture so assiduously that no one had gone hungry even in days of scarcity.

PRIESTS

During the first four dynasties of the Old Kingdom, when the personal power of pharaoh was unquestioned, we have seen that the noblemen and civil servants were completely under pharaoh's thumb. So were the members of the third important body in the social hierarchy: the priests.

At the beginning of the dynastic era there existed three distinct schools of religious thought in Egypt. The first, based on the two cities of Hermopolis (one in the Delta, the other in Middle Egypt), held that the world had been created by Thoth, scribe of the gods. The second, centred at Heliopolis (in the suburbs of modern Cairo), the City of the Sun, believed that the creator was not Thoth but the sky god Ra or

80 A priest

81 Horus and his mother Isis

Ra-Atum. The third school of priests, at Memphis, worshipped a god called Ptah, whom they regarded as the ancestor of Ra-Atum himself (*11*). And since Memphis was the royal seat of the Thinite kings of the Old Kingdom, the cult of Ptah was in a specially privileged position. More dignified and intellectual than its two rivals, which were rooted in the primitive gods of the tribe, the doctrine of Memphis enjoyed the early patronage of the pharaohs.

The sun-priests of Heliopolis, however, soon began to show some of the spirit of guile and resource that was to characterize them throughout dynastic history. They came forward with a new and convenient doctrine which they dubbed the 'Royal Doctrine'. They maintained that not only had their own god Ra-Atum been the first king of Egypt, but that Horus, the *alter ego* of every Egyptian king, was in fact a personification of Ra-Atum (*81*). They therefore became the champions of the divine legitimacy of pharaonic rule, guardians of the royal succession and watch-dogs over its purity. Small wonder that their influence steadily increased until, in the later years of the Old Kingdom, the tombs of the pharaohs were actually built in the form of sun-temples (p. 47). More, when the rigid autocracy of the Old Kingdom was finally swept away, the priests of the sun-god contrived to retain their position of ascendancy. The rise of those ecclesiastical upstarts Osiris and his sister Isis, far from harming them, was actually grist to their mill—for were not the popular pair two of Ra-Atum's eight children(*84*)? Nor were they abashed when the warrior kings of Upper Egypt elected to settle at Thebes and worship an obscure and plebeian little clan-god called Amon. The Heliopolitan priesthood, whose prestige by the time of the Middle Kingdom was unassailable, blandly tacked the name of their own august deity on to that of Amon and worshipped him as Amon-Ra(*29*).

The cult of Ra in his various aspects slowly came to constitute the official religion of the Egyptian state. But the worship of a multitude of other gods and goddesses—well over two thousand of them—did not therefore cease. The local gods continued to exist quite happily side by side with the high gods of Thebes and Memphis. The priests of ancient Egypt were not bigots or fanatics; their religion was too genial and all-embracing to breed zealots. Its forms and principles were too various and untidy for reform to be a serious proposition; and in a society which lacked a radical and progressive ethic, reformers were in any case at a discount. Thus when the pharaoh Akhenaton launched his frantic campaign against the priests of Thebes, the whole country breathed a sigh of relief when it was eventually defeated.

To attack religion was to attack life itself. Religion was not a theory, a thing apart: it penetrated at every point into the daily life of the community. The temples, as we have seen, were not merely places where religious services were performed: they were schools, universities, libraries, archives, and centres of administration and scientific enterprise; they were workshops and granaries. Nor was religion merely a matter of over-whelming economic importance: it also fulfilled its primary role of explaining, in simple and satisfying terms, the mysteries of existence. When you walk round the galleries of museums you will see the weird-looking statues of Egyptian gods, the dried-up mummies of cats and birds and crocodiles which were once objects of worship. And you may well find it difficult to imagine that such a curious religion could ever have been taken seriously. Yet the oddness and diversity of the gods was only a mirror of the oddness and diversity of life itself. If the gods were strange and marvellous, funny and terrifying, so was life. The Egyptians lived in a country where individual objects stood out against the bare bright landscape with startling clarity. They lived intensely through their sense of vision, and were more conscious of the richness and peculiarity of living creation than we are. Viewing the world with their fresh and childlike eye, it seemed to them that a divine spirit informed all things, pouring itself with incredible prodigality into an endless variety of human and animal envelopes. It could transfer itself from one envelope to another; it could live in all its envelopes simultaneously. The shining essence of Ra could flow into a falcon at the same time that it was flowing into a pharaoh, or a bull, or a *scarabaeus* beetle. The spirit was one and indivisible. Men, birds, animals, reptiles, insects and fishes were only different aspects of the life-force. That is why the Egyptian did not regard it as incongruous to go on adoring his odd-looking gods, human, half-human, or inhuman. To us they sometimes look frightening; but to him they were familiar and comforting.

There was certainly little to frighten him unduly in a religion that lacked a true sense of right and wrong. Questions of right and wrong were civil questions, not religious ones. Morality was a social and legal matter, whereas religion was mainly concerned with magic. There was no real Satan in the Egyptian pantheon to inspire constant dread and unease. Even Seth, the god of drought and storm, Lord of the Red Land, the inhospitable desert, who had murdered his brother Osiris, was worshipped. He too played his proper part in the scheme of the universe. If one approached him tactfully and in the right way, he could be truly useful and benevolent. The gods and goddesses were not considered to be unduly remote and awe-inspiring. They were grouped in families like human families—fathers, mothers, brothers, sisters, uncles and aunts and cousins. They had their ups and downs, their squabbles and reconciliations. Their shortcomings and amorous or drunken escapades were the subject of popular tales. The Egyptians treated them almost like members of their own family, as if they were carrying on their workaday activities side by side with the human inhabitants of the Nile valley. Indeed, so little feared were they that if they were slow in granting the request of their petitioners, they could be punished by the withholding of offerings, or their idols were given a sound thrashing.

If you had visited an Egyptian temple, you would have been aware that you were visiting a state within a state, like a

82 A priest and temple women in procession

mediaeval monastery. The informal atmosphere of much of Egyptian religion was reflected in the busy air of these teeming power-houses of Egyptian activity. You would not have been surprised to see ordained priests, their robes tucked round their waists, ploughing the fields, threshing the corn or tending the bees. As in the case of the Roman Catholic orders, some bodies of priests were bustling and practical, others were scholarly and contemplative. Some of the priests would be sitting cross-legged with their rows of small pupils, imparting the secrets of a smooth and well-shaped hand; others would be poring over tindery scrolls in the cool, dim House of Life, as the library was called; others would be discussing a problem in astronomy, or a novel method of dosing a fever or setting a broken limb. There were literally thousands of priests in Egypt, and together with the members of the civil bureaucracy they practised the skills which in our own society are carried on by separate professions.

Of course, however humble a priest might be, or however minor his grade, he still had a specific office to perform in the daily round of religious services. The chief celebrants of the most important rites were naturally members of the senior ranks.

83 Priests carrying a model of the sacred sun-boat in procession

The texts frequently mention four of these: the Father of the God, the Slave or Servant of the God, the Ordinary Priest (literally Pure One), and the Lector-Priest. Their main functions were to carry out the all-important Daily Rite. This was an exact imitation of the Rite of the House of the Morning, which pharaoh, the supreme priest of all, had already performed in his palace in the distant capital. The officiating priest, accompanied by his assistant priests and the women singers who were attached to every temple, solemnly broke the clay seal which had been fixed to the door of the shrine the previous day. He took the statue of the local god from its niche and proceeded to feed it, robe it in coloured clothes, rouge its face and adorn it with the royal emblems. Then he replaced it in the shrine, sealed the doors again, and left the sanctuary walking backwards, effacing his steps with a palm leaf.

Although the Daily Rite was the principal and most solemn celebration of the day, the regular duties of the priests were by no means over. The individual priest was a member of a team which worked right round the clock, dividing the hours of day and night into regular watches. Nor were the ceremonies within the temple precinct the priest's only preoccupation. He was

133

responsible for organizing and superintending the local festivals of the god, many of which were elaborate and spectacular, and went on for more than a week(*82, 83*). They included the harvest festivals of the fertility god Min at Esna and Thebes, in the second of which pharaoh himself took part; the noisy and orgiastic festival of the cat-goddess Bast at Bubastis; the boisterous anniversaries of Seth at Ombos, Denderah and Papremis; and the great annual jubilee of Horus at Buto.

In the heyday of its glory, imperial Thebes enjoyed festivals that rivalled in colour, splendour and high spirits any festivals that the world has known. The earliest of the annual festivals was the Festival of the Valley, at the height of which pharaoh crossed the Nile in his ceremonial barge to pay his respects to the shades of his ancestors in their Houses of Eternity among the western hills. Impressive though it was, this festival was eclipsed by the month-long Festival of Amon: the occasion when the images of Amon, his wife Mut and their son Khonsu were carried by water from Karnak to Luxor and, after an interval, brought back again. The festival took place during the period inundation, when the river gave the population a respite from their labours and enabled many thousands of them to crowd its banks to gape at the divine flotilla as it sailed along. If anything gives the lie to the legend of a staid and mournful Egypt, it is the sequence of these joyful festivals, when for days on end the inhabitants of town and country danced, drank and frolicked in the open air. There was a pleasant feeling abroad that the gods were also taking a rest from their exertions and were on holiday too. With a strong constitution, a modest supply of cash, and a nicely diminished sense of social responsibility, one could travel from end to end of the Black Land and find that somewhere or other there was a public holiday every day.

Undoubtedly the festivals were occasions for horse-play and junketing. They were a boon to innkeepers, souvenir-sellers, municipal treasurers and the Egyptian equivalent of hot-dog and soft-drink sellers. But there was also a genuine substratum of religious emotion. The focal point of the gaiety was the gilded image of the god as it was carried past in procession. In front of it paced the proud figures of the priests with their staffs of office, shaven-headed and naked to the waist, or clad in bright robes

84 Isis, with her brother and husband Osiris

and panther skins and wearing fantastic bird and animal masks. Around them skipped their women musicians, shaking their castanets.

It was the priests who had decided beforehand the form and duration of the festivities, and they proved themselves to be gifted pageant-masters. They were as adept at staging a popular entertainment as they were at providing their royal patrons with a useful miracle or two, by means of a talking statue or an obliging oracle. There is a case to be made for regarding the priests of Egypt as the world's first stage-producers. And their *chef d'oeuvre* was undoubtedly the great eight-act passion play in honour of Osiris which was enacted every year at Abydos. The mysteries of Osiris were also celebrated at Heliopolis, Buto, Sais, Letopolis, and at Busiris in the Delta, which was the god's original home; but it was at Abydos that the dramatic instincts of the Egyptian priesthood were given full range. The fame of the annual passion play turned the town into a combined version of Oberammergau and Bayreuth.

A synopsis of the play which has come down to us dates from the reign of Sesostris III of the Twelfth Dynasty, who ruled about 1878–43 B.C. It was committed to papyrus by a certain Ikhernofret, who had been commissioned by the king to provide an up-to-date setting of the ancient text. If, as there seems good reason to suppose, the play was already in the religious repertoire as early as the Fifth Dynasty, a full five centuries earlier, then it can claim to be the first large-scale theatrical event known to history. It was still being performed at Abydos about 550 B.C., in the closing years of the Twenty-Sixth Dynasty: a more or less continuous performance of two thousand years. Surely this must constitute something of a record run?

We saw in an earlier chapter that Abydos had come to be regarded as the chief of the holy cities of Egypt. It gradually became everyone's ambition to make a pilgrimage thither to participate in the passion play and to set up a small commemorative plaque in the sacred necropolis; and we have seen that rich men frequently left instructions for their bodies to be taken by river to Abydos for burial near 'the staircase of the great god'. In the passion play, the leading roles were assigned by pharaoh to his principal officers of state; the role of Horus, Osiris' 'darling son', was especially coveted. The majestic cycle of the life, death, mummification, resurrection and enthronement of Osiris was portrayed in scenes that occupied many successive days. The citizens of Abydos and the flood of pilgrims joined in as extras, half of them representing the partisans of Osiris and the other half those of his enemy Seth. There were magnificent progresses, and vigorous fights on land and water, alternating with tragic and pathetic episodes that culminated in the eventual triumph of the god. Max Reinhardt could not have wished for more grandiose or varied material.

There was, of course, another and totally different side to Egyptian religion, in addition to the temple liturgies and the control of day-to-day activities. This was the aspect that related to death and the dead. We have sought to show that Egyptian tombs are not the dreary, gloomy places which we might expect them to be; but the trappings of mortality can never be very cheerful to contemplate. In Egypt, the celebration of life was balanced by the celebration of death. There was a large portion of the priesthood that passed its entire existence in the service of the dead. Its members were immured in the necropolis or pyramid-city, pensioners of some prince or nobleman who had died many generations before, and who had provided for the recital of constant prayers for the repose of his soul. The great burial-grounds were virtual prisons for this sad regiment of men,

136

85 A granary
Funerary model from Sakkara, First Intermediate Period

86 Ploughing
A wooden model of the Middle Kingdom

87 Milking
From a limestone sarcophagus, Eleventh Dynasty

since the value of the grave-goods which were sealed into the sepulchre made it necessary for the cemetery-guards to maintain a 24-hour vigil.

Each day the mortuary priest would carry out a Mortuary Rite intended to be a parallel of the Daily Rite performed in the temples. In place of the image of the god, the mortuary priest removed from the shrine the image or actual mummified body of the dead man, which he placed on a mound of sand and proceeded to dress and to feed. Then he carried out the important rite of the Opening of the Mouth, when the lips of the image or mummy were touched with a sacred metal instrument. This restored to the dead man his bodily faculties and reconstituted him as a 'living soul'. And finally the priest piled on a low altar or table the regular offering of fruit, meat, bread and beer, supplemented by a libation of milk, blood or the water of the Nile. The offering was known as the 'Gift-which-the-King gives', in recognition of the intercession with the gods which the king alone had power to make, and in memory of the time when the king actually made such gifts of food to his dead favourites(85). It was the spiritualised essence of the offering that nourished the Ka and the Ba (p. 81), which flew into the chapel through the false door to receive it. What, one wonders, finally happened to this mass of food and drink? Was it thrown away? Was it treated as the perquisite of the mortuary priest? Or was it given as alms to the poor as part of a system of public relief?

88 An offering to the dead

Finally, perhaps, we ought to add a word about the process of mummification, the ingenious practice which so fascinates the modern layman and which has supplied an unfortunate symbol for the entire race. To many people the phrase 'ancient Egypt' immediately invokes the mental image of a mummy-case— another reason why the ancient Egyptians are too often mistakenly regarded as having been remote and petrified. The very word 'mummy' is wrongly applied, as it does not really refer to the dead body but comes from the word *mûmîyah*, used by latter-day Arabs to signify bitumen. The blackened appearance of the ancient cadavers misled them into supposing that the corpses had originally been dipped in pitch. This had only taken place in the final, decadent stages of the art, when it was in complete decline.

In early times the bodies of wealthy persons were wrapped in bandages soaked in natron; otherwise the dead were simply and decorously laid out in wooden coffins or placed in mat-lined pits in the sand. It was probably the warm air and the dry sand, acting as natural preserving agents, that first gave the Egyptians the idea that the physical body could be protected indefinitely from decay. Experiments were made, and by the end of the Old Kingdom a variety of ingenious modes of burial were in vogue; the earliest attested mummy (which was destroyed when the Royal College of Surgeons was bombed in 1941) appears to date from the Fifth Dynasty. The practice received a natural impetus at this period when, under the increasing influence of the cult of Osiris, pharaoh lost his unique prerogative of ascending to heaven and the privilege was extended to the citizens at large.

The priestly devotees of mummification grew more and more skilful. In their heyday they were able to offer a regular tariff for the operation, ranging all the way from a talent of silver down to a miserable handful of coppers. First the priests would pulp the brain of the dead person and draw it through the nostrils by means of a hook, in such a way as to leave the outward appearance of the face completely intact. Then they would remove the intestines through an incision in the abdomen, depositing them in four alabaster vases, specimens of which can be examined in many museums. The vases were under the individual protection of the four sons of Horus, who in turn were under the protection of four of Egypt's best-loved goddesses. The heart was wrapped separately and reinserted in the body, for it was held to be the actual seat of the intellect and emotions, and would be required when its dead owner presented it for weighing in the scales of the goddess Maat. Linen, sawdust and aromatic spices were packed into the empty abdomen, and

89 Dressed as the god Anubis, a priest completes the rite of mummification

the body was dried by means of natron applied either in solution or in dry form. It might be as long as 70 days before the corpse was considered sufficiently dehydrated to be ready for its final laving and anointing.

The bandaging now began. Rolls of linen were first steeped in gum and then moulded closely to the body. At intervals the swathing was halted to insert charms between the layers. The three charms which were most highly favoured were a large scarab of green stone (the 'heart' scarab), a red Isis fetish, and a white Osiris fetish; scraps of papyrus with magic formulae or religious texts were also tucked between the folds; and each finger and toe was bandaged separately. Often more than one layer of bandages was applied: the mummy of Tutankhamon, for example, was wrapped in no less than sixteen.

The climax of the complex and curious art was reached under the Eighteenth Dynasty, when the plumpness of life was uncannily restored to the corpse by the use of resinous pastes applied to the outside of the body. Artificial eyes were often provided, and toenails and fingers were held in place by means of thread or metal stalls. After the Twenty-first Dynasty a significant practice began to set in, symbolic of the failing condition of Egyptian civilization as a whole: less attention was paid to the embalming of the body, and the simulated appearance of outward health became all important. Gaily painted bandages and fancy swathing were all the fashion (*40, 89*).

Although the ritual of mummification remained fashionable until the advent of Christ, the methods by which it was achieved became increasingly degenerate. In the end the crudely-wrapped corpse was simply dipped in bitumen or pitch, becoming so brittle that the Copts and Arabs gleefully dug them up to snap them into small pieces for use as firewood.

More interesting and pleasing than the mummies themselves are the stone sarcophagi or coffins in which they were deposited. They were usually beautifully carved or carpentered, and covered inside and out with elaborate designs and texts, which in themselves are of the highest value to modern historians. The arrangements of the literary and pictorial motifs is usually carried out with great skill and imagination. The rendering of the face, particularly on the separate masks—called cartonnage masks—that were often fastened to the mummy, is sometimes startling in its delicacy and realism. In this respect the exquisite mummy-cases of the Greek dynasties are outstanding, for it was their standard practice to embellish them with an actual portrait of the dead person. The series of Graeco-Egyptian portraits which have survived include several which can justly be classed among the most sensitive examples of portraits ever painted.

SOLDIERS

The annals of ancient Egypt are full of wars and rumours of wars; so it cannot be said that the Egyptians did not possess a definite, if somewhat diminished, share of the aggressive instincts of mankind.

The wars that they fought, on the other hand, were such petty affairs that it is impossible to rate Egypt at all highly among the outstanding warrior nations of the ancient world. Even their major campaigns were little more than tribal skirmishes. In the 3,000 years of dynastic history we have a record of only three battles of any real magnitude: the battle of Megiddo, fought by Tuthmosis III; the battle of Kadesh, fought by Ramses II; and the naval engagement against the 'Sea Peoples' fought by the navy of Ramses III.

Tuthmosis III was certainly a gifted commander, and it would be unfair to belittle his daring exploit at Megiddo, when he executed a brilliant advance through a difficult mountain pass against the advice of his staff. But Ramses II's much-vaunted victory at Kadesh was marred by the spectacle of the Egyptian army disgracing itself, and the situation was only redeemed by the bravery of a battalion of foreign prisoners pressed into Egyptian service. Neither of these battles was on the lavish scale of a Gaugamela or a Cannae.

It may be true to say that a great warrior nation is only born as the result of a threat or challenge from another warrior nation on its borders. Thus the British and the Germans became warrior nations as a consequence of continual pressure from the French. But what pressure of this sort existed in the case of Egypt? They were not intimidated by the presence of any powerful neighbour. The Bedouins of the eastern and western deserts were simple tribesmen; the Nubians lived far to the south in their own remote fastnesses; and for most of dynastic history there was little to fear from the peoples of the eastern Mediter-

90 Syrian captives

ranean. The rise of the great nation states had not yet taken place; the desert of Sinai was an excellent natural barrier; the peoples of Palestine and Syria were small and divided, and provided a deep neutral zone between Egypt and her potential enemies. All that the Egyptians needed to do to preserve their peace and independence was to organise an efficient system of desert patrols and a strong line of protective fortresses in Nubia and the eastern Delta.

This accordingly is what they did. The fortresses which they designed bear favourable comparison with the fortresses of mediaeval Europe or the Crusader fortresses of the Holy Land. With their 20-foot brick walls, originally designed to guard the palace of the pharaoh, their massive buttresses, portcullis doorways, ramps and ditches, they were almost impossible to take by direct assault and fulfilled their defensive purpose admirably.

Great warrior nations do not spring into existence to serve a defensive function. Their *raison d'être* is aggression. If the Egyptian citizen could live in security behind his lines of fortresses, why should he bother to cultivate an offensive philosophy? He did not need to go raiding into neighbouring territories for the necessities of his existence. There was no need for him to cultivate an aggressive spirit. Thus he never absorbed the lessons of discipline and hardihood he would have had to learn if he had been constantly in a state of war.

In the Old Kingdom there appears to have been little or no military organisation on a large scale. There were small regular units for guarding supply routes, supervising work gangs and escorting expeditions to the stone or metal mines at Turah, Sinai and the Wadi Hammamat. There were also a number of semi-freelance commanders, called 'caravan leaders', who supplied bands of freebooters for special duties in the desert. Much of the patrolling of the waste lands of east and west was also undertaken by auxiliaries of an independent and almost wild character. These were the 'hunters', men who resembled the Indian scouts of the American Frontier, roaming the deserts with their tracker-dogs. They would report on the movements of the Bedouin, chase runaway criminals, prospect for gold and other minerals, and hunt for game.

At this early date there is no evidence that any large national army existed. Nonetheless, the nomarchs and local landowners had certainly begun to form their personal retinues and private armies. When the collapse of central authority occurred at the end of the Old Kingdom, the feudal barons set upon one another with their rabble at their heels; and when the civil wars were over the resolute pharaohs of the Middle Kingdom determined to abolish this particular nuisance once and for all. They abolished the pernicious system of local levies and replaced it with a properly-trained central army whose commander-in-chief was the king himself. The kings of the Twelfth Dynasty, particularly the founder Amenemhat I, Sesostris II and Sesostris III, threw themselves into the task with characteristic energy. National conscription was instituted, regiments and companies were formed, and a civilian administration was set up to keep the army provisioned. A generalissimo was appointed to act as Brigadier-General to the royal Field-Marshal, and generals were designated to take command of specialised corps. Chief among these was the Commander of Shock Troops and the Commander of Recruits.

The work of the Twelfth Dynasty was enthusiastically continued by the founders of the New Kingdom. These, the pharaohs of the Eighteenth Dynasty, were the champions of the Empire. They numbered among their ranks the most warlike of the native-born pharaohs: Tuthmosis I, Tuthmosis III, Amenophis II and Horemhab. The last-named, in fact, was a leathery old regular soldier who was called upon to salvage the state after the disastrous rule of the unbalanced genius Akhenaton. Horemhab did his task well, and handed on his sceptre to an elderly fellow-general, Ramses I, founder of the Nineteenth Dynasty. The son of Ramses I, Seti I, became another great imperial figure, who duly bequeathed an expanded Empire to his own resplendent son, Ramses II.

In the days of the Eighteenth Dynasty the balance of power in the ancient world was at last beginning to change. The populations of the Near East were breaking out of their sheltered valleys. Petty states were flexing their muscles; nomadic tribes were growing bold and predatory; other and fiercer Empires than the Egyptian were in the making. The time had come for Egypt to realise that she was part of a larger world. She must advance as far as the river Euphrates to hold the restless Mitannians at bay; she must look to the north, where the

Hittites were emerging as a new power. It was necessary for her to take action to protect herself.

At first, in the Eighteenth and early Nineteenth Dynasties, she showed herself fully capable of adapting herself to meet the new turn of events. Acting on the precept that the best form of defence is to attack, the Egyptian kings marched resolutely forward to the conquest of Syria and Palestine, establishing themselves there as suzerains(*90*). For 20 years Tuthmosis III made an annual summer campaign in Palestine, keeping the native princes in a proper state of subjugation.

These unprecedented efforts required a large and well-trained army(*92–3*). At its peak the army of Ramses II consisted of about 20,000 men, grouped in four divisions of 5,000 men each. The divisions were each named after one of the fiercer gods of Egypt, and bore his standard. Generals proliferated, and were responsible for different arms of the service: the archers, the axemen, the spearmen, the recruits, the reserve, the supply service. One important general was in charge of the 'Braves of the King', a *corps d'élite* which was expected to place itself in the thick of the fight. Regular rewards were made to officers and men who performed acts of courage. In addition to pensions and promotion, grants of land and gifts of slaves, they might also receive the 'Gold of Valour', a special insignia that was hung round their necks at a ceremony presided over by the king himself. It was an outstanding token of individual distinction.

During the period of anarchy known as the Second Intermediate Period, which intervened between the Middle and New Kingdoms, a very important event occurred: the Egyptians decided to adopt the horse. They must have known about the horse in earlier centuries, as a result of their extensive travels in the Mediterranean; but they showed no more interest in it than they did in the camel, and it played no part in their lives or their mythology. Perhaps it was considered too large and expensive to feed, and not as useful a beast of burden as the ox. Whatever the reason for the ban, it was suddenly lifted about 1700 B.C. during the reign of the Hyksôs or Shepherd Kings, the rulers of Asiatic bands who had infiltrated into the Delta and eventually subdued the whole country. Whether the Hyksôs actually introduced the horse or were themselves the recipients of it from an

Aryan source is not definitely known: but the noblemen of Egypt were soon joyfully hunting from chariots and riding races against each other. The military possibilities of chariotry, already a feature of foreign armies, particularly

91 A two-horse chariot

that of Syria, was quickly grasped. The tactic was rapidly devised of using the chariotry to make the first assault on the enemy line, with the infantry following close behind, and then wheeling aside to regroup in order to charge the enemy at the end of the battle and inflict maximum casualties. The war chariot was larger than the small private chariot, as it was pulled by two horses and was occupied by two men, the driver and the fighting man. The former plied the reins and cracked the whip, while the latter sought to protect them both with an ample shield and seized what opportunity he could to wield bow and arrow, sword and javelin. Like the private chariot, the war chariot was a light two-wheeled vehicle with a body of wickerwork, open at the back(91). Many were splendidly decorated, together with the trappings of the horses that were harnessed to them. For some reason the Egyptians seldom chose to ride astride their horses' backs, either because a nobleman considered it undignified or because the Egyptian breed of horse was too weak in the spine. So the Egyptians possessed chariotry but not cavalry.

In spite of the glory and excitement of the military life there was always widespread hostility towards it. The royal recruiting officer who made the rounds of the villages, pressing one man in ten into compulsory service, could hardly have been a popular figure. The Egyptian peasant was by instinct a man of peace. He did not thrill at the prospect of spending years of his life locked up in an uncomfortable barracks, marching up and down in step beneath the contemptuous eye of the drill-master and executing orders to the sound of the trumpet. Work in the fields was hard, but at least it was close to home.

92-3 Archers and spearmen

Schoolmasters made constant propaganda against the choice of the army as a career. The intensity and outspokenness of their satires and lampoons is astonishing, and testifies to the freedom of speech that existed under this undeniably authoritarian *régime*. The proud charioteer is represented in one composition as compelled to squander the whole of a small fortune he inherited from his parents on the upkeep of his stable and his chariot. He has an accident, and his chariot is wrecked in a ditch at the very moment when the general-in-command is making his inspection. He is arrested, sentenced to be beaten, laid on the ground and given a hundred strokes. As for the humble infantryman, the satirist paints an even gloomier picture of the wretched life he leads. His basic training is so harsh that his body is covered from head to foot in open wounds. If he resists he is beaten like a parchment. Then he is made to march over the mountains to Syria, humping his pack like a beast of burden. The weight of it dislocates his spine. He has to drink foul water and cannot sleep at night because he has to mount guard. By the time he is ready to fight the enemy he is so exhausted that he is like a feeble little bird ready to be taken in a

148

on the march

trap. And when at last he is able to return to his homeland he resembles a piece of rotten timber. He is ill, unable to use his limbs, and has to be shipped home on the back of a donkey. As a finishing touch, during the journey he is waylaid by bandits and his servant takes to his heels.

The cohorts of pharaoh looked impressive enough when they marched past the royal saluting-base. Their tasselled helmets, the blades of their long curved swords, the scales and sequins of their coats of mail shone in the sun. But in actual battle they often failed to come up to scratch. The grandiose inscriptions on the monuments, like the clasps on modern war medals, are silent about their defeats: but defeats occurred, and other sources tell us about them. Once, for example, the great Hittite king Shubiluliuma chased the shattered army of Egypt the whole of the way across Syria. And the battle of Kadesh was such a fiasco that the king of Egypt publicly revealed, and recorded for posterity, the shameful conduct of the flower of his army. 'What cowardice you have shown, my charioteers! It is impossible for me to take any pride in you.'

At Kadesh the day was saved by the courage of the Shardana,

prisoners and volunteers recruited from the 'Sea Peoples' of the Mediterranean. The 'Sea Peoples' were little better than pure pirates, the vikings of the Mediterranean; but from the Eighteenth Dynasty onwards increasing numbers of barbarians and semi-barbarians were incorporated in the Egyptian army. Perhaps the Egyptians felt that fighting was barbarians' work. Thus the pharaoh Akhenaton's bodyguard was chiefly composed of Libyans and Nubians, and the bodyguard of Ramses II was exclusively drawn from the ranks of the Shardana. By the end of the Eighteenth Dynasty even Hittites figure on the rolls of the Egyptian army.

The mercenaries could not save Egypt. They could not stiffen the will to fight of their easy-going masters. Nor was their task made lighter by the knowledge that their armaments were growing increasingly inadequate. Just as the soldiers of the Middle Kingdom had tried to stem the advance of the bronze-armed Hyksôs with copper weapons, so the soldiers of the New Kingdom were condemned to fight the invaders of the Iron Age with swords of bronze. Iron was an almost non-existent commodity in Egypt; but although the goldsmiths and metalworkers of Egypt were second to none, the Egyptians always moved more tardily than other nations into a new technological era. In the age of copper they were still in the age of stone, and in subsequent ages they managed to remain one step behind. After all, they were the Egyptians, the proud, remote, conservative Egyptians: they were not in competition with the lesser breeds in the world outside.

The result was that, when in later days the Egyptian army clashed with armies of real calibre, it was always defeated. The Ethiopians, the Assyrians and the Persians had no difficulty in crushing Egyptian resistance.

We may comfort ourselves with the thought that the capacity of one nation to beat another to its knees by force is no absolute token of superiority. The ability to fight well and to fight successfully is an enviable and often indispensable quality. But it does not take a profound knowledge of history to realise that the triumph of one nation over another is not necessarily the triumph of the civilised over the uncivilised. It was so with ancient Egypt. She did not need armies to make her mighty. In victory or in defeat she was Egypt still.

SCRIBES

If they were indifferent soldiers, the Egyptians were great administrators. The order and prosperity of the Two Lands was created by a mighty host of men armed with the stylus instead of the sword.

In a land of peasants a man who can read and write is a little king. It was so in Egypt. (For a description of hieroglyphic writing, see pp. 175–77.) 'The scribe', we are told, 'orders the destinies of everyone.' To be a scribe was 'the greatest of all the professions'. It was a profession that enjoyed great prestige. Noblemen and princes, and even pharaoh himself, allowed the sculptor to represent them squatting cross-legged on the ground with a roll of papyrus resting

94 A scribe

on their knees in the patient, attentive and honourable posture of the scribe (*94*).

The schoolmasters who derided the callings of lesser mortals urged their pupils to adopt the career of a scribe. 'Be a scribe in order that your limbs may grow smooth and your hands soft, that you may walk abroad in a white robe and that men of importance may greet you with respect.' They pointed out to their pupils that 'the profession of scribe is more profitable than any other profession. It makes you exempt from manual labour. There is no need to carry a hoe, a pickaxe or a basket, or to row in a boat. Your life will be free from care.'

One of the outstanding advantages of following the profession of scribe was that there was never any fear of unemployment. The scribe could enter the royal service, the service of a great temple, or the service of a provincial nobleman. He could serve in the personal entourage of the senior officers of state, or specialise in a particular branch of administration. He could become an authority on the law, taxation or diplomacy. If he showed a definite aptitude, he could train as an architect or an engineer, in which case he would spend his life

151

building palaces, temples and pyramids, or developing Egypt's roads, harbours and canals. In a society where there was very little social mobility, where the upper class, the artisan class and the peasant class were sharply defined and rigidly separated, the status of a scribe was definitely upper, or at the very worst upper-middle class. For the man who could read and write, and who could use his brains into the bargain, all doors were open. He could aspire ultimately to the leading post in the Egyptian civil service and become prime minister and king's vizier(78).

Because he was a scribe and a civil servant, he was not therefore condemned to a life of sedentary toil. He need not necessarily pass his time listing the contents of warehouses or compiling returns of grain. In the Old Kingdom, before the advent of a regular army, he might be deputed to take command of a troop of militia. He was also entrusted by the royal writ with the task of exploring and surveying; and a responsible civil servant was always put in charge of the expeditions and working-parties despatched to foreign countries or sent into the desert to bring back scarce commodities. Thus a high official might be ordered to travel north to Beirut, Ugarit or Byblos for resin and sacred timber; south to Nubia for ivory, frankincense, fine pelts, wild animals and dwarfs; east to Sinai for copper, malachite and turquoise; or west to the prosperous oases of Kharga and Bahariya for a consignment of choice wines. Above all the caravans shuttled ceaselessly backwards and forwards between the Nile valley and the distant quarries, there to hack out vast blocks of granite, limestone, sandstone, marble, porphyry, calcite, schist, diorite and other valuable stones. Many of these journeys were long and dangerous; but because their purpose was to secure materials which would enrich pharaoh's tomb or palace, or those of his chief courtiers, the civil servant who performed his task successfully was sure of a generous reward.

ARTISTS

Egypt's priests and pharaohs, viziers and scribes are gone: they have vanished from the human scene. It is therefore possible to discuss them with a reasonable degree of objectivity. But where the artist is concerned the case is unfortunately quite different. Our own world is full of sculptors and painters, and, because their work is familiar to us and we seem able to grasp its meaning, we assume that we are also able to understand the art of the ancient Egyptians.

Appearances, as we know, are deceptive. The artists of Thebes and Memphis were not at all like the artists of modern Paris and London. The European artist of today is a romantic, defiant figure, in revolt against society, almost an outcast from it, ready if need be to suffer poverty and privation in defence of his integrity and his vision. No greater contrast between this attitude and the attitude of the Egyptian artist could be imagined.

The Egyptian artist more nearly resembled the obscure artists who worked on our mediaeval cathedrals. They were anonymous; they were not self-assertive; they did not make a fetish of their individuality. They were bound in the service of their king, their community, and their religion. They did not regard themselves as creatures set apart or subject to a special destiny. The Egyptian painter or sculptor was simply a craftsman, the companion and collaborator of all other craftsmen. He did not think of his products as occupying a superior category to the products of, say, the goldsmith, the jeweller, the furniture maker, or the carver of ivories.

The making of a fine statue was a corporate effort. The stone must first be hewn out by the quarryman in the distant quarry. This was in itself a highly skilled operation. The quarryman had no other weapons with which to attack the stone than his soft copper chisels. He needed to possess expert knowledge of the nature and inner stresses of the rock in question in order to chip holes in the cliff-face at the correct points. He would then insert his wooden wedges, wet them with water, and wait for the sun to expand the wedges and crack the rock. To be a good quarryman is to be an artist, and the sculptor himself would often watch this clever operation; for in order to avoid the transport of unnecessarily large blocks of stone, the statues would sometimes be manufactured on the spot.

The actual sculpting of the statue was not considered a single process, but only one process among several, and that an intermediate one. The sculptor must deliver his statue to the artist who specialised in cutting hieroglyphs; who would pass it on to

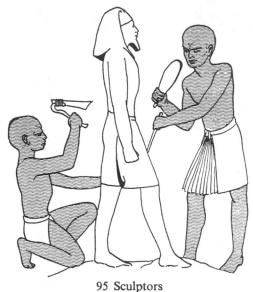

95 Sculptors

the metal worker who inserted the eyes and other details; who in turn handed it to the painter for colouring. All statues were coloured in ancient Egypt in order to make them as lifelike as possible.

The Egyptian sculptor or painter did not create his works sporadically and in response to a special mood. He did not exist on the periphery of society, but was a solid, middle-class artisan, part of a well-paid production team. If he had not been a craftsman, with objective rather than subjective standards, how could he have achieved such a consistent standard of excellence? Not for him the fitful and personal pleasures of the modern artist. He was a workman: honoured and respected, but a workman none the less. His sober professionalism was a necessary quality if he was to be able to meet the demands of his patrons not only satisfactorily but regularly, month after month, and year after year. It is astonishing, when one walks the galleries of the world's museums, to observe the sheer bulk of magnificent *objets d'art* that emerged from the workshops of Egypt. There are fine pieces not only carved in hard and soft stone, or painted on plaster, but manufactured in wood, faience, crystal, alabaster, copper, bronze, clay, ivory, and a score of other materials. And they represent only one ten thousandth part of what originally existed. Nearly all the statues and reliefs in wood, for example, which were once as numerous as the works in stone, have perished.

The rigorous training which the Egyptian sculptor underwent in order to acquire his technique is implicit in the perfect finish of his works. Some of his trade secrets—for example, how he worked certain stubborn species of stone, or cut heiroglyphs with such exactitude—have never been discovered. Evidently he served a very long apprenticeship, perhaps performing the humbler and more routine tasks of the workshop before being allowed to try his hand on more difficult ones. Throughout his career, as apprentice or master, he worked under a set of restrictions which would be incomprehensible to his modern counterpart. Thus, although he might give some rein to his fantasy in his statues of the gods (though even here most of the symbolic details were prescribed beforehand), when he made a portrait statue of a king or a nobleman he had to adhere to the literal facts. Sometimes, it is true, he was permitted to soften these facts a little, when a flabby nobleman asked to be represented as he had appeared in the pride of his youth, or an elderly princess at the height of her former beauty. But what the sitter always required was a recognizable reproduction, a kind of photograph in stone. Statues were not intended to be put in drawing-rooms as ornaments, but in tombs as objects of worship, recipients of daily offerings. They were meant to ensure the immortality of the sitter and to serve as a dwelling-place for his soul. Therefore it was essential that a statue should look as lifelike as possible; and to make its owner's identity with it doubly certain, it was stamped with his name and description. A man's name was very important to him in ancient times, not just in Egypt but in all early communities. A name was not a convenient label: it was the man himself. If one's name vanished, one no longer existed. Hence the peculiar malice of hacking a hated pharaoh's name from his monuments. It was as terrible an act as destroying his mummified body. One was obliterating him, denying that he had ever possessed the boon of life, casting him out retrospectively from the Fields of Heaven.

It must have given the Egyptian sculptor a pang when he reflected that a piece of work which he considered particularly beautiful was destined to be shut up in a dark tomb, where only a few worshippers would visit it. Probably, however, he received his chief satisfaction in making his statue effective rather than beautiful, in receiving the gifts and gratitude of his patron for executing a piece of work so lifelike that it fitted its religious purpose. There was also, of course, a whole range of sculpture that was exhibited in palaces and temples, in the open air, in the perfect light of the Nile valley. There was also a constant demand for smaller and more frivolous pieces. Our main point, none the less, is that all Egyptian statues, small or large, served a fundamental religious purpose. They were idols, fetishes, cult-objects. They were all imbued with magic. If the Egyptian sculptor was essentially a magician, then the pleasure which his statues gave could never be a purely aesthetic one.

As we have seen, Egyptian religion was neither stiff nor gloomy, and there is little stiffness or gloom in Egyptian statues. The pose is always dignified, as befits a statue made for eternity, and the attitude is poised and tranquil. But there is always a deep, slow rhythm in the wood or stone that imparts to it a human warmth. The left foot is extended a grave pace in front of the right, the arms are relaxed or gently flexed. There is no feeling of strain or tension. These were not nervous or neurotic people.

In the nature of things a statue can seldom convey any marked sense of intimacy. It was therefore left to the maker of reliefs and paintings to give us the full flavour of Egyptian life. The movement in the limestone reliefs is often extremely lively, and like the statues they were always coloured, which gave them additional animation. On the other hand there is often a tedious quality about many of the outdoor reliefs. Wall after wall of too many temples, particularly the temples of the late period, are covered with acres of repeated figures and formal inscriptions whose effect is often undeniably monotonous.

It is the surviving tomb-paintings that give us our most vivid picture of the everyday life of the Egyptians. The frescoes from the Valley of the Kings are a unique legacy from the ancient world. They depict down to the most minute detail the material life of a dead people, showing us the Egyptians at work and play, in their houses and in the countryside, in their joys and sorrows, their love for the past and their faith in the world to come(96).

Even Egyptian painting, however, presents certain difficulties to the modern spectator. Like the sculptor, the painter worked within a framework of well-defined conventions which he inherited from his early ancestors. It is one of the mysteries of human history that the civilisation of the Nile valley should

156

96 Wildfowling
From a wall-painting in the tomb of Prince Nakht, Eighteenth Dynasty

97 Girl playing a harp
Painted wooden model, Dynasty XIX

98 Female musician with a lute
Vase of the New Kingdom

have acquired most of its essential forms at so early a date, at the very onset of its 3,000-year span. The conventions which the painters of the Eighteenth Dynasty observed were already almost realised in the protodynastic palette of Narmer(4). And only a century or two after Narmer, as we can see from the decorations in the tombs of the great Thinite kings and courtiers at Abydos, the Egyptian style had finally hardened.

Many elements of this style were primitive; and it is certainly in the painting rather than in the sculpture that we can discern the primitive stratum that always underlay the crust of sophistication—though perhaps it was this cherished sense of their tribal origins which gave the Egyptians their feeling of unity and fraternity. Thus the convention of representing important people by large figures, and unimportant people by little ones, is undoubtedly primitive. So is the habit of presenting people in profile, with both shoulders turned to the viewer(96), although this convention was not, as is commonly supposed, a rigid one, as a glance at the paintings will show.

There was a reason for such conventions. It would be foolish, of course, to expect the Egyptians to have experimented with the idea of perspective. The development of perspective arrived late on the artistic scene, and was related to the scientific study of optics. But the Egyptians would not have been greatly interested in perspective even if they had known about it. They might have marvelled at it as a technical trick: but they were not really interested in technical tricks. Their conventions did not exist to give random amusement but were an expression of their fundamental modes of thought. Their conventions were realistic because they were a realistic people. The most realistic way of painting a ship, a cow, a bird or a human being was to paint it sideways on. One saw more of their essential 'thingness' that way, and there was less risk of confusion. Similarly, to a literal-minded folk the most literal way of representing 100 prisoners or 15 princesses was to paint 100 prisoners and 15 princesses, putting them in rows or registers, so that they could be easily counted, without cluttering the main theme of the picture.

For that is what Egyptian tomb- and temple-paintings really were: lists or catalogues. The frescoes in a nobleman's tomb were an exact inventory of everything he possessed, carefully tabulated so that at his death they could be transferred with him into the next world. All his wives and children were there, all his peasants, all his possessions, all his cattle and fruit-trees and cornfields and canals. They were portrayed clearly and un- mistakably. The matter was too important to permit any error.

At the same time, unless the painter was unskilful, or was executing his commission in a hurry, the catalogue was not thrown together in a grotesque and haphazard way. A man takes a pride in his family and his possessions; he wishes to see them displayed to their best advantage. Nor does the artist himself want to be sentenced to a task of stupendous boredom: he wishes to sweeten it with taste and humour. It would be vulgar of the patron to compile a mere boastful catalogue of his effects; it would be an admission of failure on the part of the artist to attempt to make nothing of his raw material. Moreover the Egyptians loved warmth and light and colour; they loved to make ingenious patterns, to achieve a balance and harmony that would mirror those qualities as they existed in Nature. The sun god Ra, standing at his zenith above the blue river, with a strip of green land and a stretch of yellow desert to left and right of him, was the outstanding and most satisfying symbol of the order and symmetry of the universe.

Like the sculptor, the painter had to undergo a long and arduous training. He had to learn the fundamental skills of making his brushes and mixing his paints. The brushes were cut from reeds, their tips carefully crushed and shaped; the paints consisted of little round tablets of resinated paste, yielding limestone for white, lamp-black or galena for black, ochre for red, and malachite and copper compounds for green and blue. The painter then underwent an exhaustive course of draughts- manship. Some of his outlines he would draw with a ruler or square or some other mechanical aid; but by dint of incessant practice he came to draw a freehand line or curve with astonish- ing fluidity. It seems safe to say that the ordinary Egyptian artist was the equal in this sphere with draughtsmen of our own era whom we consider outstanding: a Leonardo, a Holbein or an Ingres. Egyptian painters were also taught to draw their figures to scale, in accordance with a grid system which we can

study in unfinished fres-
coes. The grid was typical
of them. The Egyptians left
little to chance: thoroughness was their hallmark.

Finally the aspiring
artist, again like the sculptor, had to absorb the
spiritual as well as the
practical elements of his
trade. In much of his painting his imagination roamed
free, but there were certain
religious requirements
which he must always ob-
serve. Thus if he painted
the god Osiris, custom
dictated that he paint the
body of the god green, the
symbolic colour of resur-
rection. Amon-Ra, the sky

99 A painter

god, was painted blue, and the other gods were usually painted
yellow, to show that their flesh was made of gold. White was the
colour of hope and pleasure, red the colour of evil. The scribe
would sometimes inscribe whole passages relating to wicked gods
or wicked deeds in red; and in the Old Kingdom he would carefully score through every red hieroglyph with a black line to
neutralise the malefic influence which emanated from it.

It was not merely the tools of their craft which the scribe and
the artist shared in common. We have already noted that it was
the insertion of the written word which gave the finishing touch
to a piece of sculpture. This was also the case with a fresco,
where the hieroglyphic inscriptions were not an added embellish-
ment but were an integral part of the composition, the text of
the illustrated catalogue. Also, as we shall be discussing in the
following chapter, the hieroglyphs were pictures in themselves,
and writing the hieroglyphic language was one of the visual arts.
This free-flowing, calligraphic quality is as notable in the frescoes
as it is in the papyri and lends a supple attraction to them both.

There is a freedom about Egyptian painting which has only

been fully acknowledged during the past half-century. The pre-conceived notion that the art of this ancient people was cramped and mournful is disappearing. A glance through a volume of Egyptian painting reveals the wit and inventiveness of the Egyptian artist, and it is even becoming possible to recognise different periods and schools: for example, the austere school of Thebes in the Middle Kingdom, evolved under the influence of the stern-minded patriarchs of the Twelfth Dynasty, or the more light-hearted school of the Memphites, produced in the less astringent atmosphere of Lower Egypt. There were also a number of clearly defined regional schools, growing up beneath the patronage of the provincial nomarchs. Above all, there was the extraordinary artistic outburst of the Amarna school, when at the height of the Eighteenth Dynasty, for a period of nearly twenty years, artists were encouraged by the eccentric pharaoh Akhenaton to produce a truly revolutionary art. The fact that they could respond so swiftly to the oppor-tunity is a token of the flexibility of the Egyptian attitude to painting and sculpture.

For the fact remains that, although we have been indicating some of the limitations of Egyptian art, the artists of Egypt were also to some extent artists in our own sense of the word, just as our own artists must be to a great extent craftsmen. It would be foolish to represent the Egyptian artist as merely a factory-trained artisan. The aesthetic experience is an irreducible element in the psychic character of mankind. The Egyptian artist was closely integrated in the society in which he lived; indeed, he was immersed in it. But he was still an artist. And the spectator who takes the trouble to examine his handiwork with an open mind must become convinced of what a remarkable artist he was.

PEASANTS

The lot of the peasant was often hard: but it never seems to have become harder than he could bear. With the exception of the two terrible centuries which are called the First Intermediate Period, when the Old Kingdom broke up and the Middle King-dom was not yet established (about 2250–2000 B.C.), there is no history of peasant revolts in Egypt.

The native-born Egyptian peasant, without being a slave, was

162

a serf or bond-man. He was bound
to the service of his master and his
master's land. At the same time he
could possess land and property of
his own, and in the manner of peasants
could become prosperous. He could
own donkeys and cattle(*3, 86–7*), and
buy jewellery and fine linen for his
wife. If his existence lacked the ex-
hilaration of life in a competitive
society, it was also free from the
corresponding strain and insecurity.
He occupied his appropriate place

100 A peasant hoeing

in the world, and he knew what the king and the gods expected
of him. Since the masters of Egypt appear to have lacked any
pronounced taste for tyranny, and to have cared deeply for
the concepts of right and justice, it was possible for peasants
and masters to function together in an atmosphere of mutual
respect and esteem. It was the duty of all men, high or low, to
strive to preserve the divine order of human society. On the
peasants' broad back rested the weight of carrying out the
will of the gods. If the great god Osiris was to arise each year
from his grave in the earth, in the form of life-giving corn, it
depended as much on the peasant's labour as upon the incanta-
tions of the priests. The peasant possessed his proper dignity.

The rhythm of the seasons was the annual pageant of the life
and death of Osiris. The calendar was not a cold and convenient record of the passing of days, but a chart of the progress
of the god's martyrdom and resurrection. Osiris had been
murdered by his jealous brother Seth, with the aid of 72 accom-
plices. The body was enclosed in a casket and thrown into the
sea, but Osiris' devoted wife and sister Isis discovered it at
Byblos in Syria (suggesting a link with Tammuz, the Near
Eastern god of vegetation) and brought it back to Egypt. Seth,
enraged, wrested it from her and cut it into scores of pieces,
which he scattered throughout the length and breadth of Egypt.
The patient Isis thereupon resumed her quest, traced each frag-
ment and buried it where she found it. Most of the great Egyptian towns and temples could thus boast a relic of the god. Isis,
who had become miraculously pregnant by her dead husband

after the first discovery of his body, later gave birth to his son Horus. The birth took place in secrecy, in order to avoid the wrath of Seth, and the child was hidden in the marshes of Chemmis.

There were three seasons in the agricultural year, each divided into four months. The first season was the Season of Flood or Inundation, when the waters of the Nile reached their height. Then came the Season of Going Out, when the waters were in retreat and the crops were growing. Finally came the Season of Harvest, when the bounty of the Nile was gathered in.

The seed was sown when the waters had scarcely left the land and pools of it still stood about in the fields. Once the sun had begun to harden and bake the land, the top-soil would have been too stiff to turn. The peasants prepared their tools and kept an eye on the subsiding flood: and at the earliest possible moment they departed for the fields with their wooden ploughs and their baskets of seed corn. One man strode across the moist soil scattering the seed, while behind him followed a pair of ploughmen. One of them would guide the team and the other would lean on the handles of the plough to keep the share in the soil and throw up ridges of earth on the fallen seed. The team consisted of a pair of cows, animals which were less cumbersome than oxen to manage and strong enough to drag the light plough(86). When the ploughmen had done their work, herds of pigs and sheep were driven into the field to churn up the top-soil still further and to make sure that the seed was well puddled in. Then the surface was lightly raked over.

Many magical spells and formulae were recited during the period of sowing. Religious festivals were held, and little clay figures of Osiris in which a few seeds had first been mingled and then carefully watered were anxiously watched for signs of growth. Would the god condescend, this year, to resurrect himself?

If all went well, the crops grew tall, and peasantry were marshalled for their second great onslaught upon the land. They went forth at dawn with their sickles and laboured till nightfall in the fields, until all the ears of corn were garnered. The men cut off the ears at the top of the stalk and the women followed at their heels and put the handfuls of corn in baskets. The baskets were emptied into sacks, which in turn were transported

164

101 Harvest time: reaping and winnowing

102 A *shaduf*

to the granaries on the backs of donkeys, or by men who carried the sacks slung on long poles. The autumn days were filled with singing and laughing, and during the midday siesta there was much eating and drinking, for harvesting was hot and hungry work(*101*).

The growing of crops did not absorb all the peasant's time. There was much work to be done in his lord's garden and in his own. There were vines and vegetables to cultivate; cattle to breed; bees to tend; birds and fish to fatten. Every year the peasant must also obey a summons from the local administration to enrol in a work-gang and give a statutory number of days to carrying out the programme of public works. Roads and footpaths had to be kept in proper order, and boundary stones—which were always mysteriously shifting about—had to be restored to their rightful places. Above all, work went ceaselessly forward on the digging of new canals and the clearing of old ones. The network of the irrigation channels was the vascular system of ancient Egypt. Dykes were mended, and dams were built to conserve every last drop of the precious flood water. Water was an obsession in Egypt. From dawn till dusk peasants could be seen dipping their buckets in the well in order to replenish the square pattern of ditches in field and garden. In the New Kingdom the introduction of the *shaduf*, which raised the buckets by means of a pole, greatly lessened the tedium of the task, and the method is still used in Egypt today(*102*). But the endless task of assuaging the thirsty soil went on.

On the whole, the peasant seems to have been a happy and contented person, lithe, sunburnt and active. He enjoyed his frequent festivals, received his regular rations, and grew little luxuries for himself in his own plot of land. There were additional privileges and perquisites, among them being the custom at harvest-time of setting aside a cornfield in which

166

the peasantry were allowed to retain as much corn as they could reap in a day.

There were bad times. Osiris and Haapi, gods of the Nile, were not always generous, and the crop failed. But even then the peasant was usually safe, for he was sustained in the years of scarcity by the surpluses set aside from the good years by a wise master. Occasionally he got into trouble. He stole, or cheated on his taxes, or seduced another man's wife. Then the huge, hated Nubian policeman came to his hut, seized him and carried him before the magistrate. And if his tears and grovelling were unsuccessful, he was thrown on the ground and beaten by those same Nubian policemen. If he had done something particularly shocking, he might have his nose or ears cut off, or be sent to the chain gang or the penal settlement. On the whole, however, he was a peaceable soul, and the magistrate was usually a merciful one. There is little evidence that the more startling punishments—burning women for adultery, or throwing traitors to the crocodiles—were often carried out. Capital punishment was not a prominent feature of the Egyptian administration of justice, in spite of the fact that it existed in theory. It was such a rare event that pharaoh himself was required to review the case and confirm the sentence.

In the fine rock-cut tomb of prince Paheri at El-Kab, some of the peasants of the Nineteenth Dynasty talk to each other as they plough. 'What a beautiful mild day!' they say. 'The team is pulling well. The gods are helping us. Let us work hard for our master'. And later: 'Look how well we work! How smiling the world is! How lush the grass is growing beneath our feet!'

It would be a pity to attribute their cheerful words purely to the requirements of princely propaganda.

Chapter V

PRIVATE LIFE

THE FAMILY

THE art of ancient Egypt makes it plain that the bond between husbands and wives and their children was long-lasting and profound. Men and their wives are shown to us seated side by side in a relaxed and easy manner(*104*). The husband may have passed his arm lovingly round his wife's shoulders, while her fingers rest trustingly on his forearm. Except for the Etruscans, the married couples of no ancient civilisation are portrayed in attitudes of such obvious familiarity and affection.

Marriage was an honourable estate, a true partnership. What helped to make it so was the freedom enjoyed by the wife and the respect in which she was held. She basked in the lustre shed on her by the first wife of all, the goddess Isis, tenderest and most fruitful of ladies(*84*). It was Isis whom, we remember, journeyed as far afield as Syria and throughout the length and breadth of Egypt in order to retrieve the portions of her husband's dismembered body. There was nothing weak or feeble about Isis, and she set an example to future wives that encouraged them to be equally robust and practical. More, by performing this dangerous service for her husband she had made it possible for him to undergo his resurrection, and she was thus the indirect saviour of mankind. In some respects the prestige of the Egyptian wife possessed older antecedents even than the cult of Isis, for she enjoyed in addition the special honour accorded to her predecessors in pre-dynastic times, when women were regarded as the mysterious source of life, possessors of psychic powers beyond male experience, and guardians of the myths and traditions of the race.

True, on occasion she was required to share her position in the home with other wives, which in the nature of things must have led to stresses and strains. The king himself had an extensive *harîm*, which housed not only native beauties but the foreign

169

103 Ladies in gala dress

princesses who were sent into Egypt to become his brides. His ministers, and those in other walks of life who possessed strong nerves and deep purses, were also at liberty to marry several wives. Plural marriage must inevitably result in a certain amount of jealousy and bickering, and in the case of the royal *harîm* it could lead to intrigue and assassination. We know of at least one major crisis which was caused by a *harîm* conspiracy: the attempt to murder Ramses III, of which we possess the actual account of the trial. When the plot was revealed, Ramses ordered one of his sons to commit suicide and executed six women and forty men, including his Steward of the Harîm, his Captain of the Bowmen, his Fan Bearer and his Majordomo. Doubtless the king was subsequently led to brood on the perils of polygamy, and envied the majority of his subjects who had only a single wife to contend with.

Even in plural marriages, honour attached to the situation of the individual woman. It was not necessarily a man's firstborn son but the son first born to him by his Chief Wife who was considered his heir. The Chief Wife was a person of great consequence, the undisputed ruler of the household, and she was the legal owner of the family furniture and possessions. If she or any of her husband's minor wifes were 'put aside', should her husband choose to divorce her, generous provision in the matter of alimony had to be made to her. She also had full access to the local magistrate to beat her breast and show her bruises if her husband ill-treated her—beyond, that is, the occasional

170

104 A priest and his wife
Limestone sculpture from Thebes, Eighteenth Dynasty

105 Seated Woman. *Vase*
of the Nineteenth Dynasty

106 Womanservant grinding corn
Painted limestone sculpture, Fifth Dynasty

107 Mother and child
From a tomb-relief at Thebes, Twenty-sixth Dynasty

judicious beating that is permitted to the male spouse in Near Eastern countries.

The Egyptians were such an intensely romantic race that it seems correct to suppose that there were as many love-marriages as marriages brought about by purchase or parental negotiation. The love poems of Egypt constitute a major portion of the literary canon. They are long and ardent, and it is a pity that few of them have been rendered into English as sensitively as they deserve. Their flavour would then emerge as a blend of the rhapsodic outpouring of the *Song of Songs* with the grace and humour of Ezra Pound's transliterations from the Chinese.

The love poems do not suggest that the Egyptian husband, after undertaking a passionate courtship, was likely to develop in later years into a domestic tyrant. Clearly the virtues of gentleness and consideration were highly regarded in the relations between the sexes. The young men and young women who figure in the poems would plainly grow closer to one another in later life, until they matured at last into one of the dignified and devoted couples who hold hands on the monuments.

EDUCATION

'A splendid thing is the obedience of an obedient son', a text tells us. Another declares: 'I was one who was loved by his father, praised by his mother and loved by his brothers and sisters.'

One of the recognised ways of securing the esteem of one's father and mother is to do well at school; and lessons in ancient Egypt were serious and thorough. After the carefree days of infancy, when he shouted and larked about in the sun, the Egyptian boy was immured for long silent hours in the temple classroom—unless his parents were so wealthy that he could be educated by a personal tutor. Discipline was strict and beatings were frequent: for it was a priestly maxim that 'a boy's ears are in his backside'.

The first subjects which a boy learned were the first subjects of any advanced educational system: how to read and write. He would be instructed how to hold the wooden palette in his left hand, and how to moisten the tip of his rush pen in the pot of clear runny gum before brushing it across the dry cake of red

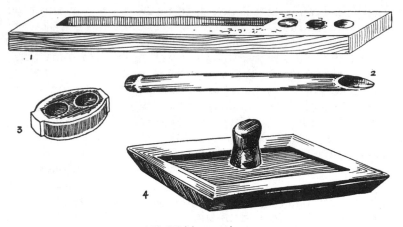

108 Writing equipment
1. Wooden pen-case   2. Reed pen   3. Inkwell
4. Black basalt palette and muller for grinding pigment

or black ink. At first he would practice on some inexpensive material: a sliver of limestone from the temple rubble heap, the smooth surface of pieces of broken potsherd, or a simple wooden board that could be wiped or scraped clean. Eventually he would copy his exercises on to a roll of papyrus. The papyrus roll had been made by cutting the fresh green stems of the sedge-like papyrus plant, peeling off the rind, laying the slices of pith across one another, then pounding and pressing them into a flat sheet before leaving them to dry. On occasion the pupil might use expensive materials provided by the tanner: rolls of vellum, parchment, and fine leather. But the common material was papyrus, which was easy and cheap to manufacture in a country beside whose waters it grew in such abundance.

As a rule the pupil would guide his rush pen horizontally across the paper from right to left, rather than from left to right. Sometimes, however, he would write up and down in columns; or even write one line from right to left and the next from left to right in the curious serpentine style known to handwriting experts as *boustrophedon*. On Egyptian monuments, of course, you will see the inscriptions carved in several different ways in the space of a small compass. This was for purposes of balance and harmony, as the lines or registers of writing were always treated as an integral element in the whole design, as they are in Japanese colour-prints.

The form of Egyptian script that is most familiar to us is *Hieroglyphic Writing*. The word *hieroglyph* comes from the Greek words *hieros* and *gluphē*—'sacred' and 'carving'. This is the form that is always used on the monuments and for formal inscriptions. It came into existence almost fully formed in earliest dynastic times, about 3000 B.C., and enjoyed a substantially unchanged existence of almost four thousand years. As the signs and pictures were difficult to write at speed, a shorthand version of hieroglyphic writing called *Hieratic* (Greek: *hieratikos*—'priestly'), was eventually evolved for writing official documents; and towards the end of the dynastic epoch there came into existence an even more rapid shorthand version of Hieratic itself: *Demotic* (Greek: *dēmotikos*—'popular'). Demotic writing was thus a kind of double shorthand of the original hieroglyphic writing.

Until the discovery of the famous Rosetta Stone by the French army in 1799 (it was subsequently 'liberated' by the British army, and is now in the British Museum), the decipherment of ancient Egyptian texts was impossible. The Rosetta Stone obligingly set out a decree of Ptolemy V Epiphanes in the three forms of writing that were current in Egypt on the threshold of the Christian era: Greek, hieroglyphic and demotic. The familiar Greek thus provided scholars, after some initial setbacks, with a key to the other two. As early as 1822 the brilliant young French scholar Jean-François Champollion had gained an insight into the true nature of hieroglyphic writing, by using the Rosetta Stone and by identifying the names of Cleopatra and Ptolemy written inside cartouches on an inscription at Philae. (Cartouches are the oval lines with a stroke at the beginning which you will see at intervals in most Egyptian inscriptions. They contain the names of kings and queens. The word *cartouche* is French for cartridge, which is what Napoleon's soldiers thought the device resembled. The hieroglyph of the cartouche actually represents a rope tied with a knot, possibly symbolic of the fact that pharaoh was owner of everything which the sun went round.)

Before his premature death, at the age of 42, the indefatigable Champollion had greatly advanced the studies of hieroglyphs and demotic, and successive generations of Egyptologists have since laid bare most of the mysteries of the ancient texts. Most of them—but not quite all: for the dead language still retains, and probably always will, a number of its secrets. For example, we do not know how the individual words were actually pronounced, even though we can read them perfectly and have a few clues from Arabic. Writing out the hieroglyphs in full, with a separate sign for each sound, would have been very cumbersome, so the scribes omitted some of the vowel sounds, most of the shorter words, and all the punctuation. They set down simply the consonants, or consonantal signs that implied a vowel. The effect of this skeletal procedure was a little as though we were to write the English sentence 'Please put the pen and the paper on the desk', in the form 'Pls pt pn ppr n dsk'. We have to guess at the nature of the missing vowels and link-words.

In fact, the Egyptians never succeeded—any more than the British or the Americans have—in rationalising certain aspects of their language. Like us, with our wildly aberrant English spelling, they never bothered. Why should they? Egyptian like English was an imperial tongue. If the foreigners wanted to read it, why should they go to any special trouble to make it easier for them? The hieroglyphic method of writing therefore remained for the whole of its long life-span an unresolved compromise between two systems: the alphabetic and the pictorial. The Egyptians succeeded in evolving a flexible alphabet of their own, using a sign to represent a sound or letter, or even a double or triple sound or letter; but because they were such a literal people they always clung to the primitive method of using pictures as well. Of all their senses, the visual sense was always the most highly developed. Thus they would write out a sentence like 'The girls run down the street' in alphabetic signs ('Grls rn dn strt') without being able to resist tacking on to the individual words little pictures depicting a girl, a person running, and a street. The innate delight which the Egyptians took in drawing can be seen in the beauty with which many of the inscriptions were carved and painted. Even the alphabetic signs themselves were not simply abstract letters, but little pictures in their own right. It was not until the Semites applied their minds to the matter that the alphabetic and pictorial strains in writing would be absorbed into a homogeneous system.

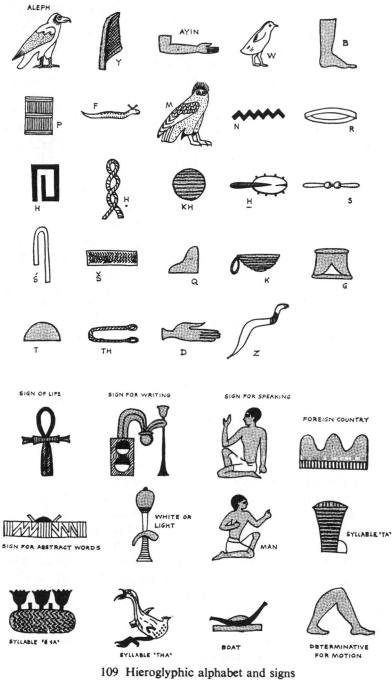

109 Hieroglyphic alphabet and signs
(*after Margaret Murray*)

These, then, were the elements of the language which the Egyptian schoolboy had to master. He was next required to practice it by copying out reams and reams of texts, mostly dry-as-dust precepts from the sayings of ancient sages which were edifying from the moral as well as the stylistic point of view. If he was lucky, he might be assigned a page or two from one of the lively and popular fictional tales. But in general his task was an unenviable one, for it must be admitted that the Egyptian author does not appear to have been as gifted or to have explored his art as systematically as the sculptor or painter or other manual craftsman. It was the plastic and visual arts which appealed most strongly to the Egyptian imagination. Some brilliant oral tradition may, for all we know, have been paramount, as in many oriental countries; but the written works, with the honourable exception of a handful of amusing tales and a cluster of poems, appeal more to the historian than to the devotee of literature. The subject matter of most of the surviving prose pieces is not exciting, and one is driven to the conclusion that the content of a story or a philosophical tract was less esteemed than the style in which it was written. The pithy sayings of viziers and wise men that make up the so-called 'Wisdom Literature' are strong, dignified and true; but we shall look in vain for the oblique insights into human behaviour afforded us by a Pascal or La Rochefoucauld. We should remember, however, that in some languages the way in which a thing is said is often more evocative than the actual thing itself, and that this may be true of Egyptian literature. When a literature with this character is translated it often seems far less interesting than it really is, for translation has deprived it of its principal virtues: the authentic sound of the words; the ring of the original phrase; the choice of metaphor; the essential rhythm and spirit. What seems trite in translation often seems lofty and magnificent in the original tongue. And we cannot even claim to know how the tongue of the Egyptians was actually pronounced. We can only say that Egyptian literature seems to contain no undisputed masterpiece of the order of the Sumerian epic of Gilgamesh, or anything to rival the literary achievements of classical China, India and Japan, or the rough glories of the Norse saga. On the whole, one does not envy the Egyptian schoolboy his task as a copyist.

178

Fortunately for his sanity, there were other subjects for him to study, subjects that probably held a greater appeal for the down-to-earth temperament of most young Egyptians. The most important of these subjects was mathematics. Our knowledge of this branch of Egyptian knowledge is not as extensive as we could wish, as our sources are scanty; but it seems evident that the science was not as advanced in the valleys of the Nile as in the valleys of the Tigris and Euphrates. The Egyptians were practical people, not metaphysicians, and had no great love of abstract thought for its own sake. They had no feeling for algebra, handled fractions in a very elementary way, and had clumsy methods of multiplying and dividing. The elusive concept of the nought (later devised by the great Arab mathematicians) evaded them, and although they invented symbols for the powers of ten, they never invented individual symbols for the numbers 2 to 9. Thus, for example, they would write the figure 13 as $10+1+1+1$; 124 as $100+10+10+1+1+1+1$; or 2352 as $1000+1000+100+100+1C0+10+10+10+10+10+1+1$.

On the other hand, they arrived at a good working knowledge of geometry, and could calculate areas and volumes in a way which would be useful to them in architecture and surveying land. They could also work out the area of a circle by measuring its diameter, and knew the properties of the trapeze and the cylinder. If their comprehension of mathematics was limited and expressed in a rudimentary and uneconomical way, they knew enough about it to suit their own purposes. They could do the calculations necessary to lay out the ground-plan of a pyramid and erect the brick ramps up which the blocks of stone were probably hauled into place(*21*): a sufficiently impressive mathematical feat. One imagines that they were in much the same position where figures are concerned as most of us today. Our ability to handle numbers tends to be sketchy: but we can usually manage to do a few simple sums on the back of an envelope that somehow seem to get us through the world all right. More than that we do not need.

The same somewhat empirical approach governed their attitude to trade. Trade appears indeed to be too grand a name for it, as exchanges were made during most of the dynastic period by means of simple barter or haggling, one object being

110 Weighing gold

swapped for another. In the late New Kingdom a gold, silver and copper standard was fairly widely operated, the weights being of metal or packets of metal dust (*110*). Two different values existed, the *deben* and the *quite*. It was now possible to express the value of an object in terms of amounts of precious metal, but the system does not appear to have become universal. The traders of Egypt were not an organised corps of middlemen or merchants in the sense in which we understand it. The Egyptian economy was predominantly pastoral and agricultural, not mercantile, and there was no well-defined middle class. The peasant or priest was his own shopkeeper. Coined money was not adopted in Egypt until the advent of Darius the Persian, at the very end of the Late Period.

Most Egyptian intellectual endeavour shared the character of their attitude to mathematics or economics. Their medicine, for example, was an odd blend of shrewdness, magic and inaccurate surmise. They became particularly expert in the sphere of bone-setting, as the great Edwin Smith Papyrus demonstrates, and were passable dentists and obstetricians. By a process of trial and error they accumulated such an extensive medicine chest that Homer called them 'a race of druggists'. It would be fair to say that the treatments they prescribed were no worse and in many respects much less alarming than those of an English doctor of two centuries ago. But the whole practice of medicine was rendered unsystematic by the widespread use of primitive spells and sympathetic magic. It may well have been the preoccupation with religion which resulted in the failure to investigate the inner workings of the body. One would have expected

180

that the complex process of embalming would have given Egyptian doctors an insight into this particular matter. An incision was actually made in the body to draw out the intestines, and the texture and appearance of the viscera must have been familiar. But the progress of an embalming was accompanied by a dense religious ritual, and the notion of using dead bodies to conduct anatomy lessons was as repugnant to the Egyptians as it was to the Roman Catholics of mediaeval or renaissance Europe.

SPORTS AND PASTIMES

It seems fitting that we should take our leave of the Egyptians in the open air. The blue sky and the golden orb of the sun were the twin symbols of their most powerful divinity, Amon-Ra, king of the gods. The Egyptians possessed a magnificent climate and took advantage of it; they loved to relax and to disport themselves.

We have mentioned that Egyptian noblemen became ardent charioteers, and horsemanship quickly established itself as a favourite upper-class amusement. The chariot was, after all, the ancient equivalent of the sports car. From the opening of the New Kingdom until the end of dynastic history, the Kings of Egypt delighted to see themselves represented in their dashing curricles, whose horses bounded along with arched backs and flashing hoofs. They held archery tournaments in which the contestants rode at full tilt past a row of oblong-shaped copper targets and loosed off at them with the bow. Amenophis II and Tuthmosis III, both enthusiasts for every variety of outdoor exercise, were expert at transfixing targets with the arrow; so was Tuthmosis III's

111 Boys wrestling

181

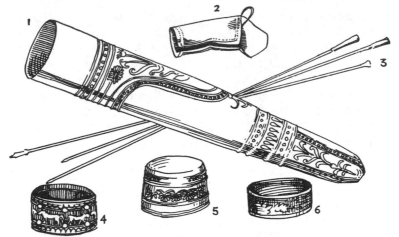

112 Hunting equipment
1. Quiver   2. Gauntlet   3. Arrows   4, 6. Dog collars   5. Quiver-lid

grandson Amenophis III, before he settled down to his long self-indulgent reign as Egypt's Caesar Augustus. The shaft of the bow which the Egyptians used in the New Kingdom was tall and straight, an improvement on the old double-curved bow which had been used in earlier times.

The Egyptian kings also liked to watch their soldiers wrestling and fighting with slaves, although these sports were too plebeian for royal participation. The art of wrestling was particularly well developed, and is depicted on many frescoes(*111*). A more aristocratic amusement was hunting, either on foot or from the chariot, and a pharaoh whose javelin wrought outstanding execution during a lion, crocodile or hippopotamus hunt would be careful to have the feat commemorated by a tablet or stele, or even by the issue of a special scarab(*72*).

Fishing and wildfowling were other universal pursuits. Nakht, a Chief Scribe of Amon during the Eighteenth Dynasty, is portrayed in his tomb in the act of hurling his curved throwing-stick at a flight of duck. He has come gliding silently down the river on one of the small boats built of bundles of papyrus, a type of boat which we have mentioned in a previous chapter. It could be made in an hour or two, and is still in use among the tribesmen of the southern Sudan. Nakht, inevitably, has been accompanied by his children. His elder daughter stands behind him, while her younger sister crouches down and clasps her father timorously round the calf. In front of him his little son, not quite aware of what is going on, brandishes his own small throwing-stick and stares enquiringly up at his father's face with his boy's long Horus-lock falling across his cheek. It is only one of a charming pro-

113 A hunting dog

cession of scenes in this memorable Theban tomb(96).

When they went hunting, the noblemen of Egypt were accompanied by their dogs. The dog had everywhere been the companion of man from prehistoric times. By the New Kingdom at least four distinct breeds, including a miniature breed, had been established. The all-purpose dog, used for work as well as diversion, was the greyhound, derived originally from a wild dog that was cousin to the wolf(113). In build it bore a distinct resemblance to the modern saluki. A more compact breed akin to the modern mastiff was also developed. The dog was fortunate

114 The *mîw*

in that it was protected by the illustrious good Anubis, who always took the form of a lean black hound. Anubis was the god of mummification and the guardian of the resting places of the departed(37). He was one of the oldest and most revered of Egyptian gods and possessed many shrines. One of the most celebrated was at Cynopolis, which the Greeks called the 'city of dogs', and where mummified dogs were carefully preserved.

The cat also enjoyed divine protection(114). In later centuries the lioness goddess Bast was more frequently worshipped in her milder guise of the cat; her principal shrine was at Bubastis. The proud and lonely cat, which the

183

Egyptians called *mïw*, took longer to domesticate than the more amiable dog, and remained in its wild state until the onset of the Middle Kingdom. Among the other pets may be mentioned the baboon and the monkey, whose mischief and drolleries have afforded mankind amusement since the beginning of history(*68*).

To conclude this brief catalogue of outdoor sports, one ought to mention the games played by children. These were as fast and strenuous, and as baffling to the onlooker, as they are today. The frescoes show us a number of games whose nature is obscure; but it is easy to recognise other pastimes that have been playground favourites from time immemorial. They include running, jumping, leap-frog, playing ball, and indulging in a kind of oriental hop-scotch(*115*). Egyptian girls, incidentally, were greatly addicted to dolls. Some of them were plain and utilitarian, but others were fine and lifelike and equipped with different sets of clothes.

The grown-up citizen would pass many hours pondering over the draught-board(*116*). The board would be placed in the living-room or under the cool shade of a tree in the garden. Boards and counters have been found in the very earliest tombs, and it seems that the players threw dice in order to control the moves

115 Girls at play

116 A game of draughts

of their black or white pieces over a board with thirty squares.

Outdoors and indoors the most frequently indulged pastime was dancing. The dance was in the main the prerogative of the women, who displayed themselves for the delectation of the men—though priests and even pharaoh seem to have performed a stately step or two during the progress of sacred festivals. The dancers were servant girls or slave girls, or perhaps little groups of professional dancers (sisters to the professional mourners at funerals) who performed at banquets(75). To judge from the tomb paintings, the dances were uninhibited and lascivious. The girls, who commonly appeared naked, pranced, shimmied, and shook their bead collars to make them rattle. Female acrobats were also much in demand, and took turns with the dancers to present their cleverly rehearsed acts(117).

117 An acrobat

185

118 Musicians at a banquet

Everywhere there was music: music at the banquet and the festival, in the streets and in the home (*118*). The orchestras were composed of both men and women, and comprised what we now called stringed, woodwind and brass instruments. The stringed instruments chiefly consisted of two kinds of harp. The larger harp was sometimes five feet tall, and possessed up to ten strings The musician sat cross-legged on the ground and supported the gaily-decorated sounding-box of the instrument on a stand. The smaller harps were light and portable, and like the larger ones were accurately tuned by means of pegs. There were many different shapes. Some of them are like the lyre, with beautifully fretted and decorated sounding boards. The string section was also supplemented by a delicate-looking lute, which commonly had four strings. Though it is usually called the lute, it is not really like the full-bellied and elaborate lute of our Elizabethan or Jacobean period; it more closely resembled a small version of the modern mandolin or guitar. A much rarer instrument was

186

the zither, a transverse harp supported on legs which was some-times heard as a novelty when foreign musicians visited Egypt.

The woodwind instruments included the mellow flute and more nasal-toned instruments resembling the oboe. There was the long single flute, usually played by men, and the small double pipe more frequently depicted in the hands of women. The double pipe had an ivory mouthpiece. The brass instru-ments were long trumpets, manufactured in bronze or copper, and were used for religious or military purposes. A famous pair, each tuned to produce a different note, was found in the tomb of Akhenaton. When blown, they gave forth the melancholy mooeing sound associated with the *lures* of Bronze Age Den-mark or the Alpine horns of modern Europe.

The Egyptian orchestra possessed a strong rhythm section. In full career it must have sounded like the rhythm section of a modern South American dance band. There were drums, several sorts of tambourine, clappers, and the characteristic

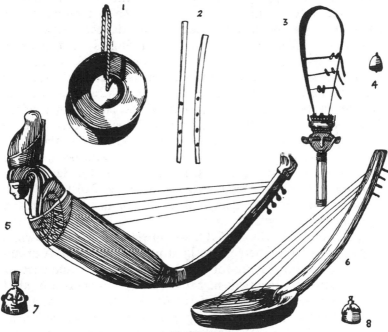

119 Musical instruments
1. *Menat* 2. Ivory flutes 3. Sistrum 4, 7, 8. Bells 5, 6. Harps

Egyptian instruments called *sistra* that were later adopted in temple rituals by the Greeks and Romans. The sistrum was a small hand-held metal instrument surmounted by the head of a cow, and between the cow's horns ran wires on which metal discs were threaded. The instrument was emblematic of the beneficent cow-headed goddess Hathor, the good and gracious wet-nurse of the pharaohs and the ruler of the sky. The sistrum was therefore of particular use in driving away evil spirits or assisting a woman in labour. When shaken gently, it would emit a soothing susurration; but it could also be shaken harshly to produce a tingling clashing sound(*119*).

A special musical effect was obtained by rhythmic clapping. The position of the hands in some of the frescoes suggests that the women in the group of musicians who were not playing an instrument were engaged in that vigorous and controlled clapping and verbal encouragement of the other performers that one hears in the flamenco groups of modern Spain. In flamenco performances clapping is an art in itself, and is as important a contribution to the musical ensemble as the thrumming of the guitar and the hammering heels of the dancers. Again, the dancers of Egypt clicked between their fingers an instrument called the *menat*, consisting of twin ovals of wood, which bore a striking resemblance to Spanish castanets. Finally, the frescoes show us the Egyptian singer performing with his hand held to his ear in the traditional attitude of the singers in modern North Africa and the flamenco singers of Spain. When we listen to the gipsy musicians of southern Spain, performing the music which is a legacy from the Moors of Africa who occupied the country for so many centuries, it may not be too fanciful to imagine that we are listening to an authentic if distorted echo of the music that once delighted those long-dead musicians in the valley of the Nile.

In the tomb of Prince Nakht, whom we watched wildfowling a page or two ago, there is a delightful banquet scene. A group of musicians are playing for the delectation of an audience of seated ladies and gentlemen. Most of the musicians are girls: but among them is an old harpist(*120*). He is blind, and seems to be plucking the strings of the harp in a muted, exalted fashion, as if for himself alone. We can overhear the words of the song, and recognise it as the longest-lived and most popular of all

Egyptian songs. It used to be sung in the far-off days of the Old Kingdom; now the old harpist is singing it a thousand years later. It will still be sung when he himself has vanished from the land of the living. It is the Song of the Harper, and in the closing lines the blind musician urges his listeners to cling to the genial philosophy which the Egyptians have always professed:

> Spend a happy day. Rejoice in the sweetest perfumes. Adorn the neck and arms of your wife with lotus flowers and keep your loved one seated always at your side. Call no halt to music and the dance, but bid all care begone. Spare a thought for nothing but pleasure: for soon your turn will come to journey to the land of silence.

120 The blind harpist

SUMMARY OF EGYPTIAN HISTORY

6000–3200 B.C.

Neolithic and Pre-Dynastic Periods
Merimdean, Tasian and Badarian cultures.
Chief sites: Pe and Hierakonpolis. Period ends
with rule of 'King Scorpion' and unification
of Upper and Lower Egypt.

3200–2700 B.C.
Dynasties I-II

Thinite, Early Dynastic or Archaic Period
Capitals: This, near Abydos, then Memphis.
Egyptian institutions evolve rapidly under
energetic rulers. Hieroglyphic writing introduced. Rival religious dogmas of Heliopolis,
Hermopolis and Memphis: Ra-Atum, Thoth
and Ptah. Building in brick and wood. Brick
mastabas. Royal Tombs of Abydos.

2700–2300 B.C.
Dynasties III–VI

Old Kingdom
Capital: Memphis. The Pyramid Age. Great
kings include Zoser (Step Pyramid), Snofru
(Dahshur Pyramids), Cheops, Chephren,
Mycerinus (Pyramids of Giza). Later, sun
temples. Triumph of religious doctrine of
Heliopolis. Egyptian colony established at
Byblos.

2300–2050 B.C.
Dynasties VII–XI

First Intermediate Period
Capitals: Herakleopolis and Thebes. Epoch of
chaos, civil war, starvation, mob violence.
Bedouin invasion. Upsurge of cult of Osiris.
Theban war-lords gain eventual supremacy.

SUMMARY OF EGYPTIAN HISTORY

2050–1775 B.C.	*Middle Kingdom*
Dynasties XI–XII	Capital: Thebes. Wise and gifted rulers: Mentuhetep I and III, Amenemhat I, Sesostris I and III, Amenemhat III. Expansion into Nubia and Asia. Literature and craftsmanship flourish.

1775–1575 B.C.	*Second Intermediate Period*
Dynasties XIII–XVII	Capitals: Thebes and Avaris. Middle Kingdom collapses: Egypt invaded by Hyksôs chieftains. Horses and chariots introduced.

1575–1085 B.C.	*New Kingdom*
Dynasties XVIII–XX	Capital: Thebes. The Empire. Great kings and queens: Ahmosis, Tuthmosis II, Hatshepsut, Tuthmosis III, Amenophis III, Akhenaton, Horemhab, Ramses II and III. Amon-Ra supreme as national god except for Akhenaton's heretical interlude at Amarna. Luxor, Karnak, Medinet Habu, Abu Simbel. Valley of the Kings. Tutankhamon's tomb.

1085–330 B.C.	*Late Dynastic Period*
Dynasties XXI–XXX	Gradual twilight of native dynasties. Country falls for periods under sway of Libyans, Ethiopians, Assyrians and Persians. Then permanently dominated by Greeks and Romans.

330 B.C.–A.D. 342	*Greek and Roman Periods*

A.D. 641	*Arab Conquest*

BOOKS FOR FURTHER READING

(Published in London, except where indicated)

ALDRED, CYRIL *The Egyptians* (1961)

CZERNY, JAROSLAV *Ancient Egyptian Religion* (1952)

EDWARDS, I. E. S. *The Pyramids of Egypt* (1960, Revised)

ELGOOD, P. G. *The Later Dynasties of Egypt* (1951)

EMERY, W. B. *Archaic Egypt* (1961)

ERMAN, A. *The Literature of the Ancient Egyptians* (1927)

FAKHRY, AHMED *The Pyramids* (Chicago, 1961)

FOX, PENELOPE *Tutankhamon's Treasure* (1951)

FRANKFORT, HENRI *Kingship and the Gods* (1948)

FRANKFORT, HENRI *The Birth of Civilization in the Near East* (1951)

GARDINER, SIR ALAN *Egyptian Grammar* (1957, 3rd edn.)

GARDINER, SIR ALAN *Egypt of the Pharaohs* (1961)

GLANVILLE, S. R. K., ed. *The Legacy of Egypt* (1942)

HAYES, W. C. *The Scepter of Egypt* (New York, 1953, 1959, 2 vols)

KEES, HERMANN *Ancient Egypt, A Cultural Topography* (1961)

LUCAS, A. *Ancient Egyptian Materials and Industries* (1948)

MONTET, PIERRE *Everyday Life in Ancient Egypt in the Time of Ramesses the Great* (1958)

PETRIE, SIR W. M. F. *Social Life in Ancient Egypt* (1924)

PETRIE, SIR W. M. F. *70 Years in Archaeology* (1931)

POSENER, GEORGES, ed. *Dictionary of Egyptian Civilization* (1962)

SMITH, W. STEVENSON *Art and Architecture of Ancient Egypt* (1958)

WHITE, J. E. MANCHIP *Ancient Egypt* (1952)

WILSON, JOHN R. *The Burden of Egypt* (Chicago, 1951)

WINLOCK, H. E. *The Rise and Fall of the Middle Kingdom in Thebes* (New York, 1947)

INDEX

Abu Simbel, Obelisk from, 48
  Smaller temple at, **19**
  Temple of Ramses II at, 38; **18**
Abydos, 34, 109, 159
  Body brought for burial at, **12**
  Osiris Mystery Play, 34, 135, 136
Acrobats, 185; **117**
Administrators, 121 ff., 151; **79**
Adoration of the Nile, hymn, 16
Agate, 93
Agriculture, 51, 163 ff.; **23, 85–7,
  100–2**
Aigyptos, 33
Akh soul, 81
Akhenaton, King, 67, 85, 130, 145,
  150, 162, 187
Alabaster lamp, **35**
  vessels, 102
Alexandria, 32
Amenemhab, courtier, Tomb of, 86
Amenemhat I, King, 118, 145
  II, 92
  III, 47, 92, 118; **76**
Amenhotep, 59, 123
Ameni, ruler of Oryx Nome, 128
Amenophis III, 51, 52, 58, 59, 67,
  123
  statues of, at Deir el-Bahri, 37
Amethyst, 93
Ammenemes III, 52
Amon-Ra, 52, 54, 60, 63, 64, 130,
  134, 161; **29**
  Temple of, 54; **27**
Amphorae, 106
Amratians, 35
Anatomy, 181
Ancestor worship, 23, 24, 78
Ani, scribe, 94
Ankh symbol, 100
Ankhesenamon, Queen, **39**
Anubis, dog-headed god, 183; **89**
  weighing a man's heart against the
  Feather of Truth, 75; **37**
Anzti, chieftain, 88
'Apis Bulls', 34
Apples, 104
Archers, 181, 182; **92, 112**

Architecture, Chapter II, 51 ff., 64;
  **10, 15, 17, 21, 24, 27, 31, 33, 34,
  36**
Army, Formation and organisation,
  of, 145 ff.; **91, 92, 93**
Arrowheads, pre-dynastic, 26; **7**
Arrows, **112**
Artists, 152–62; **95, 99**
Asheru, lake, 52
Assyrians, 32, 150
Aswan, 37, 38
  First Cataract at, 15, 82
  Harkhuf's tomb at, 122
Asyut, 126
Atbara, 38
Athribis, 32
Atlantic, 111
Auxiliaries, 144

Ba (soul), 81, 84, 139; **41**
Baer, Klaus, *Rank and Title in the
  Old Kingdom*, 122
Bahariya oasis, 152
Bak tree, 104
Bananas, 104
Barley, 107
Basketwork, 103
Bast, god, 32, 134, 183
Battles, 142, 149
Bead collar, 92; **53**
  necklace, pre-dynastic, 26; **8**
Beans, 104
Beard, false, 89
Bedouin, 143
Beds, 99, 100
Beef, 104
Beekeeping, 73, 166
Beer, 107
Beirut, 152
Bells, 187; **119**
Benben (holy stone), 47, 48
Beni Hasan, Rock tombs at, 82, 128
Bent Pyramid at Dahshur, 42
Beryl, 93
Bîbân el-Molûk (Valley of Kings),
  83, 84
Blue Crown, the (*Khepresh*), 89; **74**

193

Boats, 108; **2, 12, 72, 73**
  papyrus, 182
Boustrophedon (style of writing), 174
Bows, Bowmen, *see* Archers
Bracelets, 91, 93; **52**
Braves of the King, 146
Bread, 107
Bricks, mud, 65, 66; **30**
Bronze vessel, **61**
Brugsch, Emil, 84
Brush, paint, 160
Bubastis, 32, 134, 183
Buhen, 18
Builders, building, 64 ff.; **30**
Burial, 39 ff., 74, 140; **12, 15, 17**
Busiris, 32, 34, 37, 135
Buto, patron goddess of Lower Egypt, 89
Buto, wine district in the Delta, 32, 106, 134, 135
Butter, 107
Byblos, 70, 152, 163

Calcite, 93
Carpenters, 102; **28**
Carrots, 104
Cartouches, 175
Caskets, 103
Castor oil, 104
Cat, Domestication of the, 26, 183; **114**
Cattle, 26, 166
Cedars, 70
Ceilings, 64
Celestial Fields, The, 75, 76
Cereals, 107
Chairs, 100; **39, 66**
  carrying, 111
Chalcedony, 93
Champollion, Jean-François, 175
Chariots, 111, 147, 181; **91**
Cheese, 107
Chemmis, Marshes of, 164
Cheops, Khufu, Khufwey, 99
  Pyramid of, 45; **21**
  Sarcophagus of, 45
Chephren, King, 45, 46
Cherries, 104
Chests, 103
  pre-dynastic, **9**
Children's games, 184; **115**
Cities, Chapter II
Civil wars, 145

Cleopatra, 175
'Cleopatra's Needle', 48
Cobra as sacred symbol, 89, 92
Coconuts, 104
Coffins, 142
Coinage, 180
Collar, Bead, 92; **53**
Comb, pre-dynastic, **7**
Constantinople, 48
Copper, 26
  tools, 45, 153
  weapons, 150
Coptic monks, Destruction of ancient relics by, 29
Coptos, 35
Coral, 93
Corn, 107, 108; **101**
  grinding. **106**
Cornelian, 93
Cosmetics, 26, 94–5
Costume, *see* Dress
Couch, **66**
Court, the Royal, 114
Cowell, F. R., *Everyday Life in Ancient Rome*, 20
Crete, 17
Crowns, Pharaohs', 88; **47, 74**
  Princess's, 92; **51**
Cucumbers, 104
Cynopolis, 32, 183

Dahshur, Pyramids of, 42, 92
Dancing, 185; **75**
Darius, King of the Persians, 180
Dates, 104
Death and the Dead, Egyptian attitude to, 136 ff.; **88, 89**
Deben (weight), 180
Decoration, interior, 72
Deir el-Bahri, 84
  Temple of Mentuhotep, 36, 82
  Temple of Queen Hatshepsut, 36, 48, 51; **13**
  Tomb of Meketra, 66
Deir el-Ballas, 67, 72
Deir el-Bersheh, 66, 82
Deir Tasa, 26
Delta, the, *see* Nile
Demotic writing, 175
Denderah, 134
Devourer, the, 76; **37**
Diwan, 79

INDEX

Dog, Domestication of the, 26, 183; **112, 113**
Dolls, 184
Donkeys, **3**
Draughts, 184; **116**
Dress, 87ff.; **10, 47, 48, 50, 56**
Drugs, 180

Earrings, golden, 93; **52**
Earthenware, 102; **67**
 pre-dynastic, 27; **9**
Eating, 108; **71**
Edfu, Osiris's Temple at, 37
Edjo, Cobra-goddess, 32
Education, 173–9; **108**
Eggs, 107
Egypt, Map of, **1**
Egyptian character, 17
 language, 175
 life, continuity of, 23
 reluctance to change, 24
El-Amra, 26
El-Badari, 26
Elephantine, 37, 82
El-Qantarah, 33
Embalming, 139ff., 181; **89**
Emery, Professor, 18, 65
Enamel, 102
Ethiopians, 37, 38, 47, 150
Euphrates, 145

Faience decorations, 86, 102; **45, 46**
 goblet, **64**
Family, the, 169ff.
Fayûm, the, 26, 105
Felspar, 93
Field of Offerings, 76
Field of Rushes, 76
Fig-picking, 104; **68**
First Intermediate Period, 23, 127, 162
Fish, 105
Fishing, 182
Floors, 66
Flutes, 187; **119**
Food and drink, 103ff.; **68–71**
Foot ailments, 94
Fortresses, 44
Frankfort, Henri, *Ancient Egyptian Religion* (qu.), 25
Fry, Maxwell, 69
Funerals, 39ff., 74ff.; **12, 43, 44, 76**
Funerary model of granary, **85**

Furniture, 99ff.; **39, 65–7**

Games, Children's, 184; **115**
 Indoor, 184; **116**
Gardens, 68, 73, 103, 166; **32, 36**
Gardiner, Sir Alan, *Egypt of the Pharaohs*, 24
Garlic, 104
Garnet, 93
Gazelles, 105
Gem stones, 93
Geometry, 179
Gilgamesh, Epic of, 178
Girl playing harp, **97**
Girls at play, **115**
 with temple offerings, **26**
Giza, Pyramids of, 23, 34, 45, 60, 61; **20, 21**
Goats, 26, 105
Goblet, faience, **64**
Gods, goddesses, 32, 34, 52, 54, 63, 64, 66, 75, 113, 128–31, 161, 163, 183; **29, 37, 81, 84**
Gold, 35
 weighing, **110**
'Golden Age', 24
Gold jug, **63**
'Gold of Valour', military award, 146
Goldsmiths, 91; **52, 63**
Gourds, 104
Granaries, 73, 74; **85**
Greece, 34, 107
Greek language, 175
Gropius, 69
Gypsum, 66

Haapi, God of the Nile, 66, 167
Haematite (gemstone), 93
Hairstyles, 90, 94; **49**
Harîm, the Royal, 116, 169; **75**
 conspiracy, 170
Harkhuf, nobleman, 122, 123
Harps, 186, 188; **97, 118, 119, 120**
Harvest, 164; **101**
Hathor, Cow-goddess, 33
Hatshepsut, Queen, Temple of, 36, 51; **13**
 Obelisks of, 48, 62
Hawara, Funerary temple statue from, **76**
 Labyrinth at, 52
Head-rest, ivory, 99; **65**

195

Heliopolis, 47, 128, 129, 135
  Doctrine of, 33, 128, 129
Herakleopolis, 34, 127
Hermopolis, 128
Herodotus, 52
Hesira, Priest and Royal Scribe, 77
Hetephras, Hetep-heres, 99, 100, 102, 111
Hierakonpolis, 37, 113, 126
  Slate palette from, 4
Hieratic script, 175
Hieroglyphic writing, 151, 153, 161, 175, 176; 109
Hikuptah (Memphis), 33
Hippopotami, hunting of, 109; 72
Hittites, 32, 149
  as mercenaries, 150
Hoeing, 100
Homer, The Iliad, 35
Horemhab, soldier and builder, 57, 86, 145
Horses, 17–18, 146, 147; 91
Horus, 50, 54, 75, 88, 93, 100, 113, 129, 134, 164; 81
'House of the Morning', 113
Houses, 64 ff.; 31–4
Hunting, 109, 111, 182; 72, 112
Huntsmen, pre-dynastic, 6
Hyksôs (Shepherd Kings), 87, 147, 150
Hypostyle Hall at Karnak, 57; 27

Ibex, 105
Ikhernofret, scribe, 135
Imhotep, vizier, 41, 123; 78
Ineni, architect (qu.), 84
Intef, Tomb of, 86
Interior decoration, 72
Irrigation, 166; 102
Isis, goddess, 54, 115, 129, 163, 169; 81, 84
Ivory, 37
  head-rest, 99; 65

Jade, 93
Jadeite, 93
Jasper, 93
Jewellery, 91 ff.; 51–4
Jug, earthenware, 102
  gold, 63

Ka (soul), 81, 84, 139
Kadesh, Battle of, 142, 149

Kagemni, wise man, 123
Kahûn, 66
Karnak, 37, 51, 52 ff., 134
  Hypostyle Hall, 57; 27
  Obelisk at, 48; 22
Kemet (ancient name of Egypt), 16
Kenamon, Tomb of, 86
Kenbet (law court), 124
Khafra, see Chephren
Kharga oasis, 152
Khekheppera, scribe, 23
Khepresh (Blue Crown), 89
Khnum, ram-headed god, 32, 88, 118
Khnumet, Princess, 92
Khonsu, 54, 134
Khufu, Khufwey, see Cheops
King, Divinity of the, 60, 65
Knife, pre-dynastic flint, 27; 7

Labyrinth at Hawara, 52
Lahûn, 49, 66, 92
Lamb, 105
Lamp, alabaster, 35
Lapis lazuli, 93
Law, 124; 79
Layer Pyramid, 42
Leeks, 104
Letopolis, 32, 135
Lettuce, 104
Libya, Libyans, 150
Life-after-death, Egyptian belief in, 75, 76, 81; 37, 43
Lion symbol, 100
Literature, 178
Living quarters, middle-class, 70; 34
Louis XIV, 114, 121, 122
Love poems, 173
Lute, 186; 98
Luxor, 37, 52, 134

Maat, goddess of Truth, 75
  Hall of, 75, 88, 140
Magic, 180
Maid servant, 60
  grinding corn, 106
Malachite (gem), 93
  (cosmetic), 26
Malkata Palace, Thebes, 51, 100
Marriage, 169; 104
Mastaba tombs, 40, 45, 64; 15, 16, 77
Mathematics, 179
Meat, 104
Medicine, 180

INDEX

Medinet, Palace-temple of Ramses II at, 49, 51
Megiddo, Battle of, 142, 143
Meidum, Pyramid of, 42
Meir, 66, 82
Meketra, Chancellor, Tomb of, 66; **60**
Melons, 104
Memnon, Colossi of, 37, 51
Memphis, 17, 30, 33, 41, 117, 121, 129, 153, 162; **11**
'White Wall' of, 33, 41
Menat (castanets), 188; **119**
Mendes, 32
Menena, Tomb of, 86
Menes, King, 20
Menkaura, Mycerinus, King, 45
Mentuhetep II, 47
III, Temple of, 36, 82
Mentuhotep, vizier, 123
Merenit, Queen, 92
Meroe, 38, 39
Middle Kingdom, the, 18, 20, 23, 36, 66, 82, 106, 127, 150, 152, 162
housing, 67; **31**
Military life, Egyptian attitude to the, 147
Milk, milking, 107; **87**
Mirror, Bronze, **57**
Mittanians, 32, 145
Miw (cat), 183, 184; **114**
Money, 180
Montet, Pierre, *Everyday Life in the Days of Rameses the Great* (qu.), 19
Mortuary Rite, 139
Moscati, Sabatino, *Face of the Ancient Orient* (qu.), 18
Mother and child from tomb relief, **107**
Moufflon, 105
Mummies, 77, 139 ff., 183; **89**
Mummy-case of a priestess, **40**
Music and dancing, 185, 186; **75, 97, 98, 118**
Mut, vulture goddess, 52, 54, 134
Mycerinus, 45

Nagadans, primitive tribe, 35
Nakht, Prince, 182, 188; **96**
Napata, Ethiopian Kingdom of, 37, 38, 47
Narmer, King, 41, 94, 159; **4**

his 'White Wall' at Memphis, 33, 41
Naucratis, 32
Naval battles, 143
Necklace, 91, 93; **54**
pre-dynastic, **8**
Nectanebo II, 20
Neith, hunting goddess, 32
Nekheb, 37
Nekhebet, goddess of Upper Egypt, 89
Nems (head covering), 89
Nephthys, goddess, 54
New Kingdom, The, 20, 23, 36, 51, 74, 183
costume, 87
housing, 67
tombs, *see* Valley of Kings
New York, 48
Nile, 15, 60; **2**
Delta, 15, 16, 26, 29, 105
Towns of the, 32
Transport, 108; **72, 73**
Noblemen, 121
Noblewoman, **56**
Nomarchs, 126, 127
Nomes (districts), 82, 113, 125, 128
Nubia, Nubians, 17, 37, 39, 87, 125, 143, 150, 152, 167; **14, 59**
Pyramid tombs of, 47
Nudity, Egyptian attitude to, 90

Obelisks, 48, 62, 111; **22**
Oils, edible, 104
Old Kingdom, The, 20, 23, 34, 40, 51, 60, 75, 82, 99, 106, 121, 126, 127, 129, 140, 144, 145, 161, 162
Costume of, 87
Olive, 104
Olivine (gem), 93
Ombos, 134
Onions, 104
Onyx, 93
Opals, 93
Ornaments, pre-dynastic, **8**
Oryx, 105
Nome, 128
Osiris, 32, 34, 75, 88, 113, 115, 129, 131, 136, 161, 163, 167; **84**
Mystery Play, 135
Oxen, 104, 164; **86**

Paheri, Prince, tomb of, 167

197

Painting, 82, 85, 156ff.; **38, 96, 99**
Paints, 160
Palanquin, carrying-chair, 111
Palestine, 107, 144, 146
Papremis, 134
Papyrus, 102, 174
   The 'Smith', 180
Parchment, 174
Paris, Place de la Concorde, 48
Peaches, 104
Pearls, 93
Pears, 104
Peas, 104
Peasants, 162ff.; **100–2**
Pectorals, 92
Pendant, gold, **52**
Pepi II, 126, 127
Perfumes, 95; **58**
Peridot (gemstone), 93
Petrie, Sir Flinders, 66
Pets, 184; **114**
Pharaohs, The, 34, 113ff.; **47, 114**
   Court of, 114
   Divinity of, 60, 65
   Marriage of, 115
Phoenicia, 17
Piankhi, King of Nubia, 37
Pigs, 106
Pillars of Hercules, 111
Pittakos of Mytilene, King, 25
Plasterwork, 66
Ploughing, 164; **86**
Poetry, 173
Police, 167
Polygamy, 116, 169, 170
Pomegranates, 104
Population, 121
Pots, pre-dynastic, 27; **9**
Pottery, 102; **67**
Poultry, 105; **69**
Precious stones, 93
Pre-dynastic epoch, 25ff.; **6–9**
Priestess, mummy-case of, **40**
Priests, 50, 56, 113, 128ff.; **77, 80, 82, 83, 104**
   and the Dead, 138, 139; **88, 89**
   the power of the, 51, 60
Prisoners-of-war, **4, 90**
Ptah, god, 33, 129; **11**
Ptahhotep, vizier, 123
Ptolemy V, Epiphanes, 175
Punishments, 167
Pylons, 52, 61; **24**

Pyramids, 23, 34, 39, 41ff., 74, 111, 179; **17, 20, 21**
   economic role of the, 60

Qaw el-Kebir, 66, 82
Quite (weight), 180

Ra-Atum, 33, 47, 129, 130
Radishes, 104
Rafts, Nile, 110, 111
Ra, god, 33, 54, 113, 115, 118, 128, 129, 130, 131, 160
Ra-Harakhte, 33, 114
Ramessides, the, 83
Ramses I, 145
Ramses II (the Great), 37, 58, 85, 115, 142, 145, 146, 150; **74**
   Palace-temple of, at Abu Simbel, 48; **18**
   Palace-temple of, at Medinet Habu, 49, 51
Ramses III, 85, 143, 170
Razor, 89; **48**
Red Crown of Lower Egypt, 88
Regalia, 88, 89
Reisner, Egyptologist, 99
Rekhmira, lawgiver, 123–6
   Tomb of, 86
Religion, 75, 128ff.; **37, 80, 81–4**
Rock-crystal, 93
Rome, St John Lateran, 48
Rosetta Stone, 175
Rubies, 93

Sais, 135
Saite Dynasty, 23
Sakkara, Funerary model of granary from, **85**
   Hesira's mastaba at, **77**
   Painted sculpture from, **106**
   Royal tombs at, 40, 65, 108; **15–16**
   Step Pyramid at, 41; **17**
Sandals, 93; **4**
Sapphires, 93
Sarcophagi, 142
Sard (gem), 93
Sardonyx, 93
Saru (law court), 124, 125
Scarab, 141, 182
Schoolmasters, 148, 151
Scribe, The, 102; **94**
   the position of, 151, 192
Sculpture, 153–6; **95, 104, 106**
'Sea Peoples', The, 143, 150

INDEX

Sebakh, Sebakheen, 29
Sebennytos, 32
Second Intermediate Period, 23
Sehetepibra, vizier, 123
Sekhem (soul), 81
Sekhmet, lion-goddess, 52
Senmut, courtier, 37, 86
Serapeum, tomb, 34
Serfdom, 163
Servants, 72; **60, 106**
Sesostris I, 58
   II, 92, 145
   III, 92, 118, 135, 145
Seth, god, 105, 131, 136, 163
Seti I, 37, 58, 83, 85, 115, 145
Shadûf (well), 166; **102**
Shardana (mercenaries), 150
Shashank I, 55
Shintoism, 78
Shipping, 108–11; **72, 73**
Shrine, Garden, 73; **36**
Shubiluliuma, Hittite King, 149
Sinai, 152
Sistrum, 187; **119**
Sitamon, Princess, 100
Slavery, 61
Smith Papyrus, 180
Snofru, King, 42, 85, 99, 111
Soldiers, 142 ff.; **90–3**
Spearmen, **93**
Sphinx, the, 45; **20**
Spinach, 104
Spoon, Wooden unguent, **62**
Sports and pastimes, 181 ff.; **111, 112, 115–20**
Staircases, stairs, 72
Statues, 111, 153–6; **76, 95**
   of Amenophis III, 37
Statuettes, 82; **40, 41, 43, 59, 60**
Step Pyramid, 34, 41, 42; **17**
Stone quarries, 152, 153
Stool, **66**
Street scene, **10**
Sudan, 17
Suez Canal, 61
Superstition, 91
Sut-Hathor, Princess, 92
Sut-Hathor-Yenet, Princess, 92
Syene, 37
Syria, 17, 107, 144, 146, 147
Syrian captives, **90**

Table, **66**

Tabus, 105
Tammuz, god of vegetation, 163
Tanis, 32
Tel el-Amarna, 30, 67; **5, 10**
Temples, 36, 48, 49 ff., 82; **13, 24, 28**
   the role of the, 50
Theban tomb painting, 162; **38, 96**
Thebes, 30, 35–7, 51, 60, 67, 84, 100, 117, 123, 130, 153
   Map of, **25**
   Nomarch of, 127
   Religious Festivals at, 134
   Sculpture from, **104, 107**
This, 34, 129
Thoth, ibis-headed god, 75, 128
Ti, nobleman, hunting, 109; **72**
Titles, 122, 123
Tjel, 33
Toilet equipment, 71, 89, 94–5; **48, 55, 57, 58, 62**
Tomb paintings, 82, 85, 156; **38, 96, 99**
   robbers, 45, 74, 78, 84
Tombs, 40 ff., 74 ff.; **15, 17, 44, 77**
   Decoration in, 82, 85, 156; **38, 44–6, 107**
   rock-cut, 82, 83; **44**
Towns, Chapter II, **10**
Trade, 17, 179; **110**
Transport, 108 ff.; **72, 73**
Tura, Royal limestone quarries at, 41
Turks, 61
Turnips, 104
Turquoise, 93
Tutankhamon, 85, 99
   Chair of, **39**
   Mummy of, 141
   Ushabti of, **42**
Tuthmosides dynasty, 61
Tuthmosis I, 74, 83, 84, 145
   III, 36, 48, 85, 142–6, 181
   Obelisks of, 48, 59
Tutu, wife of Ani the scribe, toilet case of, 94; **55**

Ugarit, 152
Unguent, 70
   spoon, **62**
   vase, **59**
'Unique Friend' (title of honour), 123
Uraeus (sacred cobra emblem), 89, 92

Uronarti Island, 67
Ushabti, figurines, 82; **40, 41, 43**

Valley of the Kings, 47, 77, 83, 156
    the Queens, 77
Van der Rohe, Mies, 69
Vases, **59, 98, 105**
Vegetables, 104
Vellum, 174
Vessel, Bronze, **61**
Villa, Country, 68; **32–4**
Vines, 104, 106, 166; **70**
Viziers, 123 ff., 152; **79**

Wall paintings, 82, 85, 156; **38, 96, 99**
Water, 166; **102**
    jars, 70
Weapons, 150; **6, 7, 92, 93, 112**
Weights, 180; **110**
Wheat, 107, 108, 164; **101**
White Crown of Upper Egypt, 88; **47**

Wife, Position of the Chief, 116, 170
Wigs, 89
Wildfowl, 105
Wildfowling, 182; **96**
Wilson, J. A., *The Burden of Egypt* (qu.), 18
Windows, 57, 71
Wine, 106; **70**
    jars, 106; **70**
Women's dress and toilet, 90, 91, 94; **49, 50–6, 71, 103**
Wooden models, **85, 86, 97**
    panel from mastaba, 77
    statuettes, **59, 60, 78**
Wood, Scarcity of, 70
Wrestling, 182; **111**
Writing, 151, 173, 174; **94, 108**

Zazat (law court), 124, 125
Zither, 187
Zoser, King, 33, 121, 123
    Step Pyramid of, 34, 41; **17**
    Vizier of, Imhotep, **78**

A CATALOG OF SELECTED
DOVER BOOKS
IN ALL FIELDS OF INTEREST

A CATALOG OF SELECTED DOVER
BOOKS IN ALL FIELDS OF INTEREST

CONCERNING THE SPIRITUAL IN ART, Wassily Kandinsky. Pioneering work by father of abstract art. Thoughts on color theory, nature of art. Analysis of earlier masters. 12 illustrations. 80pp. of text. 5⅜ x 8½.   23411-8

ANIMALS: 1,419 Copyright-Free Illustrations of Mammals, Birds, Fish, Insects, etc., Jim Harter (ed.). Clear wood engravings present, in extremely lifelike poses, over 1,000 species of animals. One of the most extensive pictorial sourcebooks of its kind. Captions. Index. 284pp. 9 x 12.   23766-4

CELTIC ART: The Methods of Construction, George Bain. Simple geometric techniques for making Celtic interlacements, spirals, Kells-type initials, animals, humans, etc. Over 500 illustrations. 160pp. 9 x 12. (Available in U.S. only.)   22923-8

AN ATLAS OF ANATOMY FOR ARTISTS, Fritz Schider. Most thorough reference work on art anatomy in the world. Hundreds of illustrations, including selections from works by Vesalius, Leonardo, Goya, Ingres, Michelangelo, others. 593 illustrations. 192pp. 7⅛ x 10¼.   20241-0

CELTIC HAND STROKE-BY-STROKE (Irish Half-Uncial from "The Book of Kells"): An Arthur Baker Calligraphy Manual, Arthur Baker. Complete guide to creating each letter of the alphabet in distinctive Celtic manner. Covers hand position, strokes, pens, inks, paper, more. Illustrated. 48pp. 8¼ x 11.   24336-2

EASY ORIGAMI, John Montroll. Charming collection of 32 projects (hat, cup, pelican, piano, swan, many more) specially designed for the novice origami hobbyist. Clearly illustrated easy-to-follow instructions insure that even beginning papercrafters will achieve successful results. 48pp. 8¼ x 11.   27298-2

THE COMPLETE BOOK OF BIRDHOUSE CONSTRUCTION FOR WOODWORKERS, Scott D. Campbell. Detailed instructions, illustrations, tables. Also data on bird habitat and instinct patterns. Bibliography. 3 tables. 63 illustrations in 15 figures. 48pp. 5¼ x 8½.   24407-5

BLOOMINGDALE'S ILLUSTRATED 1886 CATALOG: Fashions, Dry Goods and Housewares, Bloomingdale Brothers. Famed merchants' extremely rare catalog depicting about 1,700 products: clothing, housewares, firearms, dry goods, jewelry, more. Invaluable for dating, identifying vintage items. Also, copyright-free graphics for artists, designers. Co-published with Henry Ford Museum & Greenfield Village. 160pp. 8¼ x 11.   25780-0

HISTORIC COSTUME IN PICTURES, Braun & Schneider. Over 1,450 costumed figures in clearly detailed engravings–from dawn of civilization to end of 19th century. Captions. Many folk costumes. 256pp. 8⅜ x 11¾.   23150-X

THE BEST TALES OF HOFFMANN, E. T. A. Hoffmann. 10 of Hoffmann's most important stories: "Nutcracker and the King of Mice," "The Golden Flowerpot," etc. 458pp. 5⅜ x 8½.   21793-0

FROM FETISH TO GOD IN ANCIENT EGYPT, E. A. Wallis Budge. Rich detailed survey of Egyptian conception of "God" and gods, magic, cult of animals, Osiris, more. Also, superb English translations of hymns and legends. 240 illustrations. 545pp. 5⅜ x 8½.   25803-3

FRENCH STORIES/CONTES FRANÇAIS: A Dual-Language Book, Wallace Fowlie. Ten stories by French masters, Voltaire to Camus: "Micromegas" by Voltaire; "The Atheist's Mass" by Balzac; "Minuet" by de Maupassant; "The Guest" by Camus, six more. Excellent English translations on facing pages. Also French-English vocabulary list, exercises, more. 352pp. 5⅜ x 8½.   26443-2

CHICAGO AT THE TURN OF THE CENTURY IN PHOTOGRAPHS: 122 Historic Views from the Collections of the Chicago Historical Society, Larry A. Viskochil. Rare large-format prints offer detailed views of City Hall, State Street, the Loop, Hull House, Union Station, many other landmarks, circa 1904-1913. Introduction. Captions. Maps. 144pp. 9⅜ x 12¼.   24656-6

OLD BROOKLYN IN EARLY PHOTOGRAPHS, 1865-1929, William Lee Younger. Luna Park, Gravesend race track, construction of Grand Army Plaza, moving of Hotel Brighton, etc. 157 previously unpublished photographs. 165pp. 8⅞ x 11¾.
                                                                                                                23587-4

THE MYTHS OF THE NORTH AMERICAN INDIANS, Lewis Spence. Rich anthology of the myths and legends of the Algonquins, Iroquois, Pawnees and Sioux, prefaced by an extensive historical and ethnological commentary. 36 illustrations. 480pp. 5⅜ x 8½.   25967-6

AN ENCYCLOPEDIA OF BATTLES: Accounts of Over 1,560 Battles from 1479 B.C. to the Present, David Eggenberger. Essential details of every major battle in recorded history from the first battle of Megiddo in 1479 B.C. to Grenada in 1984. List of Battle Maps. New Appendix covering the years 1967-1984. Index. 99 illustrations. 544pp. 6½ x 9¼.   24913-1

SAILING ALONE AROUND THE WORLD, Captain Joshua Slocum. First man to sail around the world, alone, in small boat. One of great feats of seamanship told in delightful manner. 67 illustrations. 294pp. 5⅜ x 8½.   20326-3

ANARCHISM AND OTHER ESSAYS, Emma Goldman. Powerful, penetrating, prophetic essays on direct action, role of minorities, prison reform, puritan hypocrisy, violence, etc. 271pp. 5⅜ x 8½.   22484-8

MYTHS OF THE HINDUS AND BUDDHISTS, Ananda K. Coomaraswamy and Sister Nivedita. Great stories of the epics; deeds of Krishna, Shiva, taken from puranas, Vedas, folk tales; etc. 32 illustrations. 400pp. 5⅜ x 8½.   21759-0

THE TRAUMA OF BIRTH, Otto Rank. Rank's controversial thesis that anxiety neurosis is caused by profound psychological trauma which occurs at birth. 256pp. 5⅜ x 8½.   27974-X

A THEOLOGICO-POLITICAL TREATISE, Benedict Spinoza. Also contains unfinished Political Treatise. Great classic on religious liberty, theory of government on common consent. R. Elwes translation. Total of 421pp. 5⅜ x 8½.   20249-6

PHOTOGRAPHIC SKETCHBOOK OF THE CIVIL WAR, Alexander Gardner. 100 photos taken on field during the Civil War. Famous shots of Manassas Harper's Ferry, Lincoln, Richmond, slave pens, etc. 244pp. 10⅝ x 8¼.   22731-6

FIVE ACRES AND INDEPENDENCE, Maurice G. Kains. Great back-to-the-land classic explains basics of self-sufficient farming. The one book to get. 95 illustrations. 397pp. 5⅜ x 8½.   20974-1

SONGS OF EASTERN BIRDS, Dr. Donald J. Borror. Songs and calls of 60 species most common to eastern U.S.: warblers, woodpeckers, flycatchers, thrushes, larks, many more in high-quality recording.   Cassette and manual 99912-2

A MODERN HERBAL, Margaret Grieve. Much the fullest, most exact, most useful compilation of herbal material. Gigantic alphabetical encyclopedia, from aconite to zedoary, gives botanical information, medical properties, folklore, economic uses, much else. Indispensable to serious reader. 161 illustrations. 888pp. 6½ x 9¼. 2-vol. set. (Available in U.S. only.)   Vol. I: 22798-7
Vol. II: 22799-5

HIDDEN TREASURE MAZE BOOK, Dave Phillips. Solve 34 challenging mazes accompanied by heroic tales of adventure. Evil dragons, people-eating plants, blood-thirsty giants, many more dangerous adversaries lurk at every twist and turn. 34 mazes, stories, solutions. 48pp. 8¼ x 11.   24566-7

LETTERS OF W. A. MOZART, Wolfgang A. Mozart. Remarkable letters show bawdy wit, humor, imagination, musical insights, contemporary musical world; includes some letters from Leopold Mozart. 276pp. 5⅜ x 8½.   22859-2

BASIC PRINCIPLES OF CLASSICAL BALLET, Agrippina Vaganova. Great Russian theoretician, teacher explains methods for teaching classical ballet. 118 illustrations. 175pp. 5⅜ x 8½.   22036-2

THE JUMPING FROG, Mark Twain. Revenge edition. The original story of The Celebrated Jumping Frog of Calaveras County, a hapless French translation, and Twain's hilarious "retranslation" from the French. 12 illustrations. 66pp. 5⅜ x 8½.
22686-7

BEST REMEMBERED POEMS, Martin Gardner (ed.). The 126 poems in this superb collection of 19th- and 20th-century British and American verse range from Shelley's "To a Skylark" to the impassioned "Renascence" of Edna St. Vincent Millay and to Edward Lear's whimsical "The Owl and the Pussycat." 224pp. 5⅜ x 8½.
27165-X

COMPLETE SONNETS, William Shakespeare. Over 150 exquisite poems deal with love, friendship, the tyranny of time, beauty's evanescence, death and other themes in language of remarkable power, precision and beauty. Glossary of archaic terms. 80pp. 5³⁄₁₆ x 8¼.   26686-9

THE BATTLES THAT CHANGED HISTORY, Fletcher Pratt. Eminent historian profiles 16 crucial conflicts, ancient to modern, that changed the course of civilization. 352pp. 5⅜ x 8½.   41129-X

THE STORY OF THE TITANIC AS TOLD BY ITS SURVIVORS, Jack Winocour (ed.). What it was really like. Panic, despair, shocking inefficiency, and a little heroism. More thrilling than any fictional account. 26 illustrations. 320pp. 5⅜ x 8½. 20610-6

FAIRY AND FOLK TALES OF THE IRISH PEASANTRY, William Butler Yeats (ed.). Treasury of 64 tales from the twilight world of Celtic myth and legend: "The Soul Cages," "The Kildare Pooka," "King O'Toole and his Goose," many more. Introduction and Notes by W. B. Yeats. 352pp. 5⅜ x 8½. 26941-8

BUDDHIST MAHAYANA TEXTS, E. B. Cowell and others (eds.). Superb, accurate translations of basic documents in Mahayana Buddhism, highly important in history of religions. The Buddha-karita of Asvaghosha, Larger Sukhavativyuha, more. 448pp. 5⅜ x 8½. 25552-2

ONE TWO THREE . . . INFINITY: Facts and Speculations of Science, George Gamow. Great physicist's fascinating, readable overview of contemporary science: number theory, relativity, fourth dimension, entropy, genes, atomic structure, much more. 128 illustrations. Index. 352pp. 5⅜ x 8½. 25664-2

EXPERIMENTATION AND MEASUREMENT, W. J. Youden. Introductory manual explains laws of measurement in simple terms and offers tips for achieving accuracy and minimizing errors. Mathematics of measurement, use of instruments, experimenting with machines. 1994 edition. Foreword. Preface. Introduction. Epilogue. Selected Readings. Glossary. Index. Tables and figures. 128pp. 5⅜ x 8½. 40451-X

DALÍ ON MODERN ART: The Cuckolds of Antiquated Modern Art, Salvador Dalí. Influential painter skewers modern art and its practitioners. Outrageous evaluations of Picasso, Cézanne, Turner, more. 15 renderings of paintings discussed. 44 calligraphic decorations by Dalí. 96pp. 5⅜ x 8½. (Available in U.S. only.) 29220-7

ANTIQUE PLAYING CARDS: A Pictorial History, Henry René D'Allemagne. Over 900 elaborate, decorative images from rare playing cards (14th–20th centuries): Bacchus, death, dancing dogs, hunting scenes, royal coats of arms, players cheating, much more. 96pp. 9¼ x 12¼. 29265-7

MAKING FURNITURE MASTERPIECES: 30 Projects with Measured Drawings, Franklin H. Gottshall. Step-by-step instructions, illustrations for constructing handsome, useful pieces, among them a Sheraton desk, Chippendale chair, Spanish desk, Queen Anne table and a William and Mary dressing mirror. 224pp. 8⅛ x 11¼. 29338-6

THE FOSSIL BOOK: A Record of Prehistoric Life, Patricia V. Rich et al. Profusely illustrated definitive guide covers everything from single-celled organisms and dinosaurs to birds and mammals and the interplay between climate and man. Over 1,500 illustrations. 760pp. 7½ x 10⅛. 29371-8

Paperbound unless otherwise indicated. Available at your book dealer, online at **www.doverpublications.com**, or by writing to Dept. GI, Dover Publications, Inc., 31 East 2nd Street, Mineola, NY 11501. For current price information or for free catalogues (please indicate field of interest), write to Dover Publications or log on to **www.doverpublications.com** and see every Dover book in print. Dover publishes more than 500 books each year on science, elementary and advanced mathematics, biology, music, art, literary history, social sciences, and other areas.

BAKER COLLEGE LIBRARY

3 3504 00459 6971

DT 61 .W48 2002
White, Jon Ewbank Manchip,
1924-
Everyday life in ancient
Egypt

BAKER COLLEGE OF CLINTON TOWNSHIP
34950 LITTLE MACK AVENUE
CLINTON TOWNSHIP, MI 48035

1. Most items may be checked out for two weeks and renewed for the same period. Additional restrictions may apply to high-demand items.

2. A fine is charged for each day material is not returned according to the above rule. No material will be issued to any person incurring such a fine until it has been paid.

3. All damage to material beyond reasonable wear and all losses shall be paid for.

4. Each borrower is responsible for all items checked out on his/her library card and for all fines accruing on the same.

DEMCO